Simple Sewing

PROJECTS

make it™ Yourself

Simple Sewing PROJECTS

Quick-stitch designs for sewing by hand and machine

weldon**owen**

Pincushions & Notions

Purses, Bags & Accessories

For Kids & Pets

Holiday Projects

Basics & Patterns

LOOKING FOR A QUICK FIX to perk up a room—a new throw pillow or blanket, innovative storage ideas, or something to brighten up a wall? Maybe a small gift to give to a little one or your favorite furry, four-legged family member? Or a personalized way to tote your belongings to work, school, or around town? With fabric, needle, thread—and just a little time—you can whip up all of those things and much more. *Simple Sewing Projects* features a broad array of fresh designs for machine sewing, hand sewing, and simple embroidery. Nearly every project can be made in a weekend—many in a single day or just a few hours. A few no-sew projects even capitalize on the magic of fabric glue and other time-saving products. So hit the fabric store and have some fun!

the Editors

Pillows & Throws

Brighten up the living areas throughout your home with handmade pillows, blankets, and throws that look better than store-bought.

OO1
craft a honeycomb pillow

This nature-inspired pillow comes together with a little machine stitching and simple hand sewing.

YOU WILL NEED
10×14-inch pillow form
2—11×15-inch felt rectangles
Pencil
Cardstock
Felt sheets
Pins
Disappearing fabric marker

1. Draw a 2×2-inch hexagon on cardstock to use as a template. Cut out shapes in a variety of colors to create a pleasing design (A).

2. Using pins, attach the hexagon shapes to the pillow front, leaving the centers free and small gaps between each shape. Mark a seam line down the center of each row (B) and machine-stitch using neutral-color thread. With right sides together, sew the pillowcase, leaving a 5-inch gap on one side to insert the pillow form. Turn the pillowcase right side out, insert the pillow form, and whipstitch the opening closed with matching thread.

A

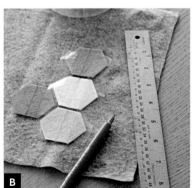

B

felt facts

There's so much more to felt than primary colors and flimsy rectangles. Today's felt is made from acrylic, wool, bamboo, or rayon blends and is sold off the bolt and by the sheet. It's also available in a variety of thicknesses, from 2 to 10 millimeters. If you can't find the right felt for your needs at local crafts or fabrics stores, hit the Web. Our favorite sources for beautiful felt include commonwealthfelt.com, purlsoho.com, and thefeltpod.com.

002
piece a pillow

Fashion a large throw pillow by combining four fabrics for a dazzling diamond effect.

YOU WILL NEED

¾ yard of fabric 1 (pillow top, piping)

⅓ yard of fabric 2 (pillow top)

1 yard of fabric 3 (pillow top and back)

¼ yard of fabric 4 (pillow top)

Rotary cutter and cutting mat

Acrylic rotary cutter ruler with 45-degree line

3 yards of ⅜-inch cording

Polyester fiberfill

Finished Pillow: 24×24 inches

CUT THE PIECES

Fabric 1: Cut two 6⅞-inch squares; cut each in half diagonally for four triangles total. From remaining fabric, cut enough 2½-inch-wide bias strips (cut diagonally across the fabric) to total 106 inches.

Fabric 2: Cut four 4¾×18⅛-inch rectangles.

Fabric 3: Cut four 4¾×18⅛-inch rectangles and one 24½-inch square.

Fabric 4: Cut two 6⅞-inch squares; cut each in half diagonally for four triangles total.

1. Align 45-degree line on acrylic ruler with a corner of a fabric 2 rectangle and trim (Diagram 1). Repeat at opposite end to form a trapezoid. Repeat with remaining fabric 2 and fabric 3 rectangles.

2. Using ¼-inch seam allowance, sew together a fabric 1 triangle, fabric 2 trapezoid, fabric 3 trapezoid, and fabric 4 triangle (Diagram 2). Press seams in one direction. Repeat to make four blocks.

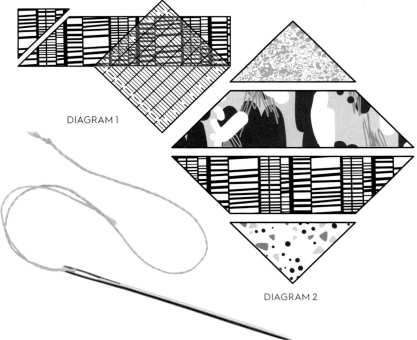

DIAGRAM 1

DIAGRAM 2

3. Join blocks in pairs (Diagram 3). Press seams in opposite directions. Join pairs to make pillow front. Press seams in one direction. To make it easier to turn corners with piping, round each corner slightly.

4. Sew together fabric 1 bias strips to make one long strip. Fold under 1 inch at one end of strip, then fold in half lengthwise with wrong side inside. Insert cording next to folded edge, placing cording end 1 inch beyond fabric folded end. Using zipper foot, sew through both fabric layers right next to cording to make piping (Piping Diagram). Trim seam allowance to ¼ inch.

5. Aligning raw edges, baste piping around edge of pillow top; begin stitching 1½ inches from piping's folded end. At each corner, gently ease piping into place around corner. Cut end of cording so it will fit snugly into folded opening at beginning. The ends of the cording should abut inside covering. Refold bias strip so it covers cording, lapping folded end over raw end. Finish stitching piping to pillow top.

6. Using basting line as a guide for stitching, sew together pillow top and 24½-inch square from fabric 3, leaving an opening for turning.

7. Turn right side out, stuff with fiberfill, and hand-stitch closed. (See Magic Invisible Closure, right.)

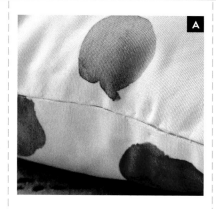

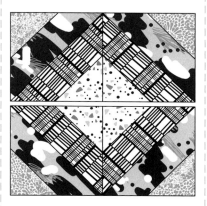

DIAGRAM 3

Piping is made by sewing a bias-cut fabric strip around a length of cording.

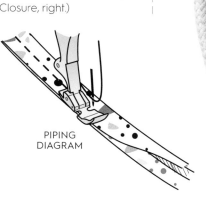

PIPING DIAGRAM

MAGIC INVISIBLE CLOSURE

Here's how to sew a seam opening closed so that the stitches are nearly invisible. Use this technique—called the ladder stitch (A)—on pillows, toys, bag linings, or anything else you need to close a seam with hand stitches.

1. Fold the seam allowances to the inside; press.

2. Thread needle with sturdy thread. Make knot at end.

3. Hide knot in seam allowances. Bring needle up at beginning of opening.

4. Insert need into first folded edge and take a small stitch (just a little bit of fabric); pull needle through fabric.

5. Insert needle in opposite folded edge directly across from position where needle came out of first folded edge. Take another small stitch; pull needle through fabric.

6. Return needle to first folded edge; take another small stitch and pull needle through fabric. Continue in this manner to make a few stitches from side edge to side edge.

7. Pull thread snugly to close opening. Secure thread end with a backstitch or two. Trim the thread, leaving a short tail.

003
create a care-free garden

Transform old wool sweaters into a free-form garden-inspired pillow.

YOU WILL NEED
80% wool sweaters in assorted colors
Liquid dishwashing soap
Embroidery floss
Embroidery needle
Pillow cover and insert

1. To felt, add sweaters to a washing machine set to hot wash/cold rinse; add a small amount of liquid dishwashing soap. Add a few lint-free items, such as old T-shirts or jeans, to provide friction as machine agitates to promote felting. If desired, remove sweater pieces two or three times during wash cycle and rinse in cold water, squeezing out excess liquid; extreme temperature changes help to speed felting process.

2. Remove sweaters before entire spin cycle is complete and roll in a towel to remove excess water. Shape and air-dry. Repeat felting process until sweaters are dense and thick. Let dry; trim excess fuzziness with scissors.

3. To create flowers, cut a series of four-petal blooms in desired sizes from the felted sweaters.

4. Secure stacked petals in graduated sizes to a plain pillow cover using French knots (see #092).

5. Sew yarn stems using a running stitch (see #092). Repeat to make additional flowers and stems across the front of the pillow cover. Insert pillow and close to finish.

004

put a photo on a pillow

Turn a plain pillow into a modern cushion in minutes.

YOU WILL NEED
Photo of vintage floral fabric
Fabric ink jet sheet
Pillow
Hot glue or fabric glue
Permanent marker
4 Pom-poms
Hand-sewing needle
Sewing thread

1. Snap a photo of vintage floral fabric (or use a child's artwork). Upload it onto your computer and print onto a fabric sheet with an ink-jet printer.

2. Trim the image as needed and secure to the pillow with hot or fabric glue.

3. Draw on scallops with a permanent marker (or glue or sew on fabric trim).

4. Sew decorative pom-poms onto the corners to finish.

005

embellish with pretty ruffles

Easy-to-sew ruffles add dimension to a pillow in a matter of minutes.

YOU WILL NEED

Linen fabric cut into 2-inch-wide strips

Coordinating thread

Hand-sewing needle

Patterned pillow cover

Pillow insert

1. Gather the linen strips and stitch in place onto the front of a patterned pillow cover in overlapping rows.

2. Fill with a pillow insert to finish.

006
add a flower to a pillow

The three-dimensional rosette starts with pieces cut from dyed felt or wool. The pieces are cut into half circles, then stitched into overlapping circular rows to form the pretty flower pattern.

YOU WILL NEED

Assorted white and cream felt or wool sweater pieces

Fabric dye powder in desired colors (we used Rit Dye powder)

Bucket

Drop cloth

½ yard of muslin

Sewing machine or hand-sewing needle and sewing thread

1⅛-inch-diameter covered button kit

20-inch square white pillow

1. Cut wool sweaters into large pieces, omitting seams. Felt the pieces (see Steps 1 and 2 of #003).

2. Following package instructions, prepare dye bath in bucket on drop cloth. Wet wool or felt. Place wool in bucket. Stir constantly for 10 to 30 minutes. Rinse wool until water runs clear. Repeat for each color. Wash and dry.

3. Cut forty 3½-inch-diameter circles from lighter-color wools and twenty-five 2½-inch-diameter circles from medium to darkest wool. Cut all circles in half. Cut one 15½-inch-diameter circle from muslin. Sew wool half circles side by side on muslin circle with round edges facing out, overlapping rows and adding darker shades of wool as you work your way toward the center. Cover button with dark wool; sew to flower center. Hand-stitch flower to pillow.

007
turn old sweaters into a new throw

Toss old wool sweaters in the washing machine to felt, then turn them into a cozy, pieced throw.

YOU WILL NEED

Old wool sweaters

Liquid dishwashing soap

Matching sewing threads

Seam stabilizer

36-inch-wide felted wool fabric

Pinking shears

Yarn and large-eye needle (optional)

Finished Throw: 41½×55 inches

FELT SWEATERS

1. Gather sweaters that are at least 80-percent wool. The number of sweaters needed will depend on desired size of finished throw and size of sweaters after shrinkage. (We used approximately 12 sweaters for this throw.) Use sweaters with patterns or designs for interest.

2. Sort sweaters by color. Place sorted sweaters, turned inside out, into washing machine. Felt the sweaters (see Steps 1 and 2 of #003).

3. Repeat felting process until stitches are no longer visible. Felted sweaters should be dense and thick. If knitted stitches show more than you like, repeat process. If necessary, hand-felt for additional firmness and smoothness by rubbing item on a washboard with hot water and liquid dishwashing soap or rolling it between palms. Let dry; trim excess fuzziness with scissors.

4. Remove sleeves from sweaters and cut along inner arm seams to lay flat. Cut body of sweater along side

and shoulder seams. Lay felted pieces on a flat surface to cut shapes needed.

ASSEMBLE THROW

1. Decide on colors to use for stripes and sort felted pieces into color groups. Our 41½×55-inch throw, shown above, consists of two horizontal rows of red-tone stripes and three horizontal rows of green-tone stripes. For each stripe, cut ten 4¼×11-inch rectangles from felted sweater pieces.

2. Lay rectangles on a flat surface, making five rows with 10 rectangles in each row. When pleased with the arrangement, sew rectangles together in rows. Sew with right sides up, slightly overlapping first rectangle with second. Referring to photograph at right, cover overlapped area with seam stabilizer and sew close to edge of top rectangle. Remove stabilizer according to package directions. Continue adding rectangles in this

manner to complete each row. Sew rows together in same manner, alternating colors.

3. Cut six 2½×36-inch binding strips from the felted wool fabric. Join short ends of binding strips. Press seams open. Fold in half lengthwise to make 1¼-inch double-fold binding. Aligning raw edges, join binding to throw using sewing machine. Turn folded edge of binding to throw back and hand-stitch in place. (For details on binding, see #094.)

—Make in Minutes—

A plain purchased pillow goes from bland to grand with the addition of running-stitch borders and a perky fabric yo-yo topped with a covered button.

008
perk up a pillow

Change the floss and fabric colors as you like to make the perfect accessory for your home.

YOU WILL NEED

17-inch square toss pillow
Water-soluble marking pen
Acrylic ruler
Embroidery floss: taupe and coral
Embroidery needle
7-inch circle of coral print fabric
1-inch-diameter covered button kit
3-inch square of brown print fabric
Spray bottle filled with water

1. Using a water-soluble marking pen and an acrylic ruler, draw a line 2 inches from the right edge of pillow that extends from top edge to bottom edge. **Note:** To get a straight line, flatten pillow as much as possible with the ruler as you draw. Draw a second straight line 2 inches from bottom edge that extends from left-hand edge to right-hand edge.

2. Draw two more parallel lines that are 1 inch apart and 1 inch inside each of the drawn lines from Step 1.

3. Using six strands of embroidery floss and a running stitch, stitch the four outer- and innermost drawn lines along the side and bottom of pillow with taupe floss (see #092). Stitch the center lines with coral floss.

4. Thread a needle with matching or neutral thread and tie a knot about

6 inches from the end. With the 7-inch coral print circle facedown, turn raw edge of circle a scant ¼ inch toward circle center. Take small, evenly spaced running stitches near folded edge. End stitching next to the starting point; do not cut the thread.

5. Gently pull thread ends to gather folded edge until it forms a gathered circle. Knot thread ends to make a yo-yo. Trim thread.

6. Referring to photo for placement, hand-stitch yo-yo to pillow.

7. Follow covered button kit manufacturer's instructions to cover button with 3-inch square of brown print fabric.

8. Sew button to center of yo-yo with matching sewing thread.

9. Lightly mist fabric with water to remove any visible water-soluble marking pen lines.

009

cross-stitch a pillow

Shades of pink, coral, and gold create an ombré effect on this pillow.

YOU WILL NEED

Graph paper

Pencil

Purchased pillow cover with loose weave

Embroidery floss

Embroidery needle

1. Plot a design on graph paper (we planned for ½-inch-wide cross-stitches), poke a hole in the center of each X, then lay the paper on a purchased pillow cover.

2. Transfer the pattern by marking each hole on the fabric.

3. Cross-stitch the design, working the rows from dark to pale hues of floss.

010
stitch pretty leaves

We used a sunflower leaf to create this pattern, but any leaf will do. Try hosta, maple, or linden.

YOU WILL NEED
Leaves
½ yard white outdoor fabric
Water-soluble marking pen
Embroidery hoop
Embroidery floss and needle
Pillow form

1. Gather your supplies (A). We used a sunflower leaf. Any leaf with an interesting shape will work.

2. Cut two pieces of fabric 1 inch longer and wider than your pillow form. Our pillow form was 18×18 inches, so we cut two 19×19-inch squares. On one piece, trace leaves using a water-soluble marking pen (B).

3. Using the embroidery hoop, floss, and needle, begin stitching around the leaf shape. We used a split stitch. Start with one straight stitch that's about the length of a grain of rice, then bring your needle up through the underside of the fabric to split the strands of floss in the original stitch (C). Continue until you've stitched around the entire shape.

4. Using embroidery floss that is a shade lighter, create a thicker outline by placing a second row of split stitches just inside the original (D). Follow the same instructions as in Step 3. Repeat for all leaf shapes on your pillow. When finished, sew the embellished square to the plain square to create a pillow cover.

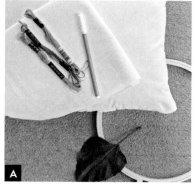
A

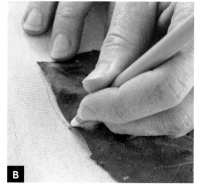
B

C

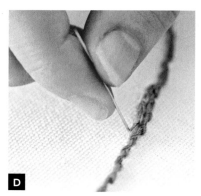
D

011
embroider a botanical print

With its spindly form and distinctive blooms, the sarsaparilla plant comes to life in textural stitches.

YOU WILL NEED

Natural linen (plain weave or twill): one 24 inch square (pillow front) and two 16×20-inch rectangles (pillow back)

8-inch embroidery hoop

Crewel wool thread: 1 skein each of Appleton #441, #442, #443, #445, #481, #992

Chenille needle: size 24, or comparable crewel needle

White cotton fabric for lining: one 20-inch square and two 16×20-inch rectangles

Hand-sewing needle

Sewing thread

18-inch square pillow form

Tracing paper

Fabric pen or pencil

Straight pins

Ruler

1. Enlarge and trace the pattern on next page onto the center of the linen square. Hoop the pillow front.

2. Refer to the diagrams and instructions in #092 (for split stitch see #010, Step 3). Stitch the stem and branches using chain stitch with #445. Split-stitch the leaves, alternating the uses of #441, #442, and #443. Stitch each blossom using circular couching stitch and #992 (see diagrams, next page) and double-wrapped French knots on the ends. Use quadruple-wrapped French knots and #481 for the flower centers.

3. Block your finished crewelwork according to Blocking 101 directions on the next page.

4. Trim 2 inches from each side of the pillow front, leaving a 1-inch border on all sides. The linen fabric with finished crewelwork should now measure 20×20 inches.

5. Lay your crewelwork facedown on a flat surface. Lay the 20-inch square lining piece on top of crewelwork. Pin the two pieces of fabric together and baste with sewing thread and hand-sewing needle, using a series of 1-to 2-inch-long straight stitches in diagonal rows spaced about 3 inches apart. Stitch loosely so stitches will be easy to remove later; set aside.

6. Lay one 16×20-inch linen rectangle on a flat surface. Place one of the 16×2-inch lining pieces on top of the linen rectangle. Pin together and baste as described in Step 5. Repeat for the second piece of pillow back and lining fabric.

7. For each pillow back piece, fold one long edge 1½ inches in toward the lining. Press with a hot iron or finger-press. Fold in again another 1½ inches, press, and pin along the folded edge.

8. Using sewing thread, blanket-stitch along the inside folded edge on each of the back pieces. Remove the pins. You should now have two 13×20-inch pieces of basted, lined, and hemmed fabric that will be used to make the backing for your pillow.

9. Lay your basted and lined crewelwork faceup on a flat surface. Lay one of the small pieces facedown

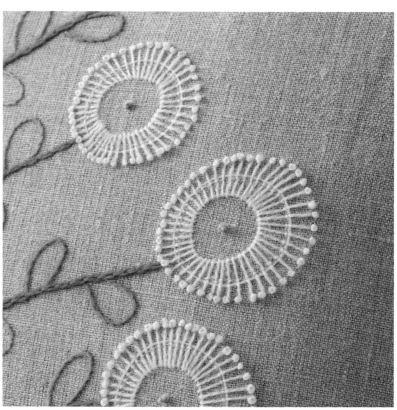

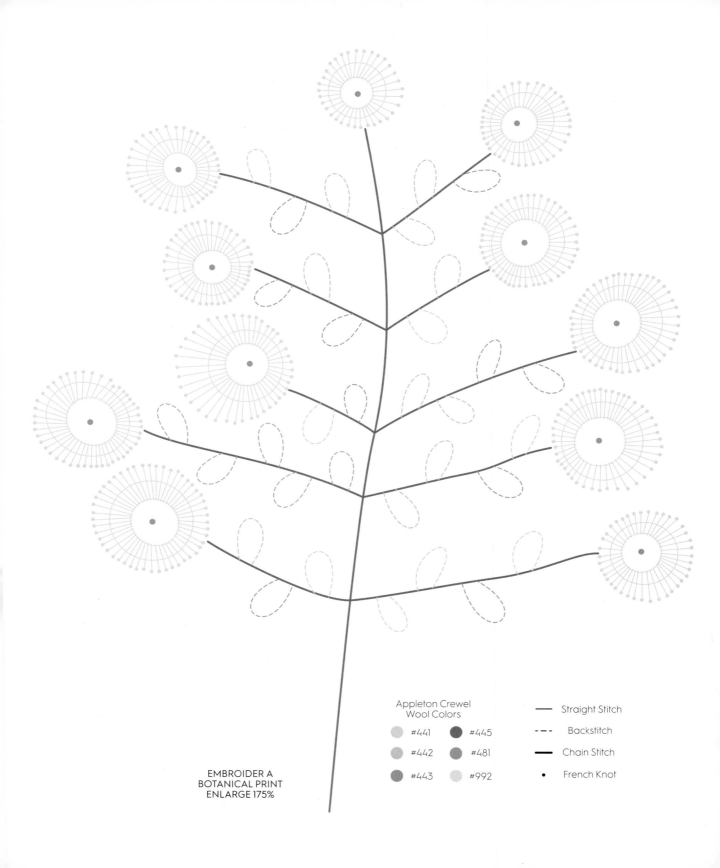

Appleton Crewel
Wool Colors

#441   #445
#442   #481
#443   #992

——— Straight Stitch

- - - Backstitch

━━━ Chain Stitch

• French Knot

EMBROIDER A
BOTANICAL PRINT
ENLARGE 175%

on top of the crewelwork with the fold in the middle and the left edges lining up. Pin the left edges together. Lay the other small piece in the same manner, matching the right side edges of the crewelwork; pin edges together. The two folded and hemmed edges now overlap in the center.

10. Pin the top and bottom edges and place a few pins through the center where the two smaller pieces overlap. Flip your work so the lining side of the crewelwork is facing up.

11. Machine-sew the three pieces together, leaving a 1-inch seam allowance on all sides; remove pins.

12. Trim the seam allowance to ½ inch. Snip corners, being careful not to cut too close to the seam; remove the basting stitches. Turn the pillow right side out.

13. Using the end of a blunt scissors, a knitting needle, or chopsticks, gently push out corners from inside the pillow. Slip the pillow insert into the opening in the back of the pillow cover and adjust as necessary.

CIRCULAR COUCHING STITCH

1. To make a circular couching stitch, stitch a series of straight stitches that shares the edge of an arch or circle.

2. Lace thread underneath straight stitches and pull it to form a circle.

3. Bring your needle up next to the center of one of the straight stitches, bring the thread over the straight stitch, and then go back down on the other side of the stitch to tack down the straight stitch. Repeat on each straight stitch.

4. Lace the thread underneath each straight stitch, outside the stitches from Step 3.

5. Pull thread to form an outer circle.

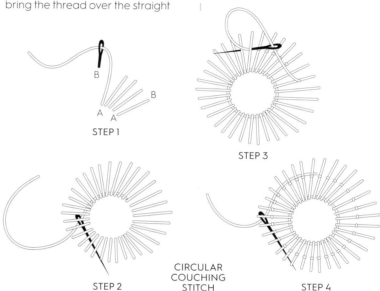

STEP 1

STEP 2

STEP 3

CIRCULAR COUCHING STITCH

STEP 4

blocking 101

This technique helps to return your work back to its correct proportions and square off the sides.

You'll need a clean board at least ¾ inch thick and larger than your finished embroidery; a piece of sturdy white cotton fabric about 8 inches wider and longer than your piece of wood; a box of 1-inch round-head, rustproof nails; a staple gun and staples; and hammer.

Wrap the board with the cotton fabric, stapling all raw and folded edges to the underside of the board.

Lay your finished embroidery faceup and centered on the board. Starting in the center of the top edge of your crewelwork, tack a nail through the linen into the board. Only about ¼ inch of the nail needs to go into the wood.

Smoothing the fabric with your hands and stretching it as necessary, tack another nail through the center of the bottom edge. Do the same in the center of the left and right edges. Working from the centers to the corners, alternating top to bottom and then left to right, nail down all edges of the embroidery. The spaces between the nails should be about 1 inch.

Be sure to keep the design square while you work. This may require stretching and pulling if your needlework lost its shape during embroidering.

Next, spray your finished needlework with cold water until it is completely soaked. Set the board in a warm, airy place to let the needlework dry. When your work is dry, remove the nails with a hammer or pliers. Your work is now blocked and ready to be framed or sewn.

—Make in Minutes—

Add personality to a plain purchased pillow with a monogram that requires zero sewing skills.
The simple method completes the transformation in minutes.

012
personalize a pillow

YOU WILL NEED

17½-inch square aqua velvet pillow cover

6-inch-tall letter stencil

Water-soluble marking pen

Assorted buttons ranging in size from ⅜-inch- to 1-inch-diameter: various shades of pink

Hot-glue gun and glue sticks

Cleaning cloth

17-inch square pillow form

Sewing needle

Sewing thread

1. Position letter stencil approximately 3 inches from left-hand edge and 3 inches from bottom edge of pillow. Using water-soluble marking pen, trace letter onto pillow front.

2. Hot-glue buttons inside letter in a random manner until entire letter is filled with buttons. Hot-glue a second layer of buttons as desired.

3. Use a damp cloth to remove any visible trace lines to finish. Stitch cover closed as needed. (You can also make a similar effect by sewing all of the buttons in place if preferred.)

013
decorate a store-bought blanket

A simple felting technique embellishes a warm wool throw with colorful snowflakes.

YOU WILL NEED
Tracing paper
Pencil
Colorful wool felt
Needle felting tool and mat
Cream-color wool throw
Sewing needle
Sewing thread
Craft beads
Plaid wool fabric for binding

1. Trace the snowflake patterns below. Enlarge and use the patterns to cut snowflakes from wool felt. Cut as many as desired for the throw.

2. Using directions on the needle felting tool and mat package, felt snowflakes to random positions on throw, using the photo as a guide.

3. Using needle and thread, embellish snowflakes with craft beads as desired.

4. Bind throw edges with bias-cut plaid wool fabric in desired width.

ENLARGE 300%

014
make a pillow pop with color

Customize a pillow to brighten a neutral space with this simple technique.

YOU WILL NEED

⅝ **yard of solid white fabric**
¼ **yard of solid red fabric**
14×14-inch square pillow form
Embroidery floss: white

Finished Pillow: 14-inch square

Measurements include ¼-inch seam allowances unless otherwise indicated. Sew with right sides together unless otherwise stated.

CUT THE PIECES

From solid white, cut:
4—4½-inch squares
2—1½×12½-inch strips
2—1½×14½-inch strips
2—9½×14½-inch rectangles

From solid red, cut:
5—4½-inch squares

1. Refer to Diagram 1 to create plus sign block.

2. Sew a 1½×12½-inch strip to the top and bottom of plus sign block (Diagram 2). Press seams toward center. Add a 1½×14½-inch strip to each side edge of block. Press seams toward center.

3. Using two strands of white embroidery floss, stitch running stitches ¼ inch inside outer edges of red squares of the plus sign block.

4. Turn under ¼ inch along one long edge of each solid white 9½×14½-inch rectangle; press. Turn under same long edges ¼ inch again; press. Topstitch folded edges to hem pillow back pieces.

5. Overlap hemmed edges of pillow back pieces about 3½ inches to make a 14½-inch square. Stitch across overlaps to make pillow back.

6. Layer pillow top and pillow back with right sides together. Stitch around all edges to make pillow cover. Turn right side out through opening in pillow back; press. Insert 14-inch-square pillow form to complete pillow.

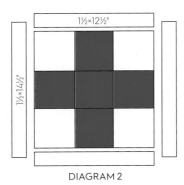

DIAGRAM 1

DIAGRAM 2

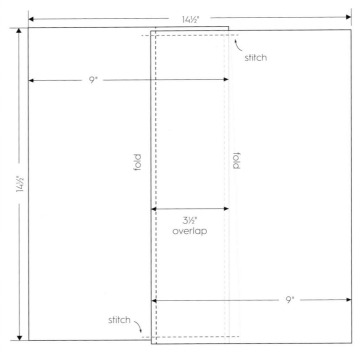

PILLOW BACK ASSEMBLY DIAGRAM

015
perk up a room with pom-poms

Make a purchased throw a little more fun by adding jumbo pom-poms to the edges.

YOU WILL NEED

Clover Pom-Pom Maker

Yarn

Scissors with sharp tips

Throw

1. Gather your materials (A). Open both arms of the pom-pom maker. Beginning at the end of one arm, wind yarn around the arm toward the hinge. Continue winding yarn onto second arm, working from the hinge to the end of the arm (B). Trim yarn to separate from ball.

3. Close the pom-pom maker (C). Hold the pom-pom maker firmly in one hand. Using the tips of the scissors, snip through the side of the yarn wraps. Use the groove in the side of the tool as a guide for the scissors (D).

4. Cut a length of yarn. If your pom-pom will be attached with a hanging string, cut a generous length. Wrap the yarn around the pom-pom maker, inserting it into the groove in the side of the tool. Tie the yarn in a single knot. Pull the yarn ends firmly to tighten the knot (E). Tie again to secure. Open the pom-pom maker arms (F).

5. Pull the center of the tool apart and remove the pom-pom (G). Trim yarn tails with scissors, leaving long tails for attaching (H). If needed, shape the pom-pom with scissors.

6. Pin the yarn tails along the edge of the throw, roll the hemmed edge to enclose the tails, and topstitch.

A

B

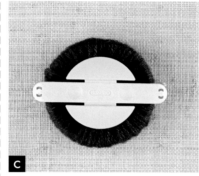

C

D

E

F

G

H

Home Decor & Accessories

Layer custom accents into each room in your home for a decorating style that's purely your own—and enjoy using your sewn creations every day.

O16
stitch a fluffy pouf

Add function and a burst of color to your house with a custom pouf.

YOU WILL NEED

Paper

Tape

2 yards of 54-inch-wide linen burlap

1 old, light solid-color bedsheet, any size (or 3 yards of 45-inch muslin)

Straight pins

Sewing machine

1 spool (125 yards) heavy-duty/ upholstery thread to match burlap

2 large garbage bags full of fabric items for stuffing (old clothing, worn towels, fabric scraps)

1 5-pound box of fiberfill

1 roll fusible-web tape

Large embroidery or straight upholstery needle

4 skeins embroidery floss to match or contrast fabric.

1. Copy the patterns on Pattern Pages R and S. Cut out the shapes. Using tape, piece together the larger pattern. When the pattern is pieced together, it will look like a rectangle with a triangle on each end (A).

2. Layer the burlap over the bed sheet. Pin the pattern into place and cut out; repeat until you have eight

sets (B). You will have eight pieces of burlap and eight pieces of bed sheet. Using the endcap pattern, cut the octagon pieces for the top and bottom of the pouf. For each piece, fold a piece of burlap in half, pin the long edge of the endcap pattern along the fold, and cut out. Repeat to make the second octagon piece..

3. Sew your pouf starting with the large long shapes. Layer one bed sheet piece on the bottom, two pieces of burlap in the middle, and one piece of sheet on top. Pin the layers together along one side. Repeat to create three more layered sets (C).

4. Using a straight stitch and a ½-inch seam allowance, sew along the pinned side of a layered set, removing pins as you sew, to create pairs of panels. Repeat with the other pinned sets (D).

5. Open each sewn set in the middle. Press the seam allowance of each pair open so a strip of burlap lies flat on either side (E, shown on the next page).

6. Lay one joined pair on top of another with right sides together (burlap to burlap) and pin. Sew along the pinned edge, unpin, and press open. Repeat with the other

two layered sets (F, shown on next page). At this point, you will have two pouf halves. Turn one half right side out and the other half inside out.

7. Nest one half inside the other with right sides together and pin around the outside edges. Make a mark 5 inches on each side of center point where all seams meet on one end of the pouf (G, shown on next page).

8. From one 5-inch mark, stitch around the outside edge of the pouf, stopping at the 5-inch mark on the other side, leaving a 10-inch opening. Reinforce the opening by sewing across the seam allowance at a right angle to the seam at the 5-inch marks (H, shown on next page).

9. Turn the pouf right side out with the opening at the top. Sort fabric scraps into heavy, light, and small piles. Start

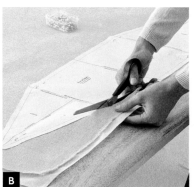

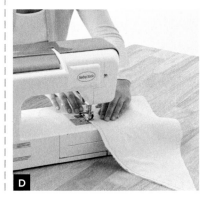

stuffing the pouf with the largest/heaviest pieces of fabric at the bottom center of the pouf. Heavy fabrics, such as denim, should be stuffed in as neatly as possible to avoid creating large gaps in the stuffing. Once the pouf is filled about halfway, use softer and smaller pieces to stuff along the sides. A

E

wooden spoon may be helpful to stuff pieces in place. Continue filling with heaviest fabrics in the center and lighter/smaller pieces around the edges. The bottom of the pouf and the center should be stuffed with the heaviest fabrics to ensure good support. The lighter fabrics should go on the outside to give a smooth finish to the poof (I).

10. When the pouf is about two-thirds stuffed, use fiberfill along the sides to fill in bumps and to smooth the shape. The tighter the pouf is stuffed, the better it will hold its shape (J).

11. Once you are satisfied with the amount of stuffing, use upholstery thread and a needle to hand-sew the seam together. The octagon piece will cover this part of the seam, so don't worry about neatness (K).

12. Using fusible-web tape to secure fold and following manufacturer's instructions, press in the edges ½ inch on all sides of the two octagon burlap pieces (L).

13. Line up the eight corners of the octagon piece with the eight seams on the top of the pouf as closely as possible. Insert pins straight down at the seams to make adjusting the alignment of the octagon easier. Using a basting stitch 1 inch inside the edges of the octagon, baste one octagon piece to the top of the pouf. Repeat on the bottom of the pouf with the other octagon piece.

14. Following our stitching how-to (next page), sew the decorative finish along the seams of your pouf. Although the stitch is simple, try practicing on a scrap of cloth to get

F

H

J

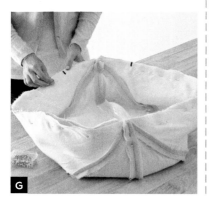

G

I

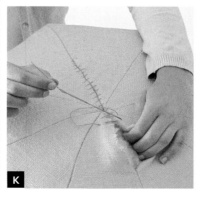

K

comfortable with the rhythm of the stitch and to perfect your technique.

DECORATIVE STITCH HOW-TO

1. Use the decorative stitch along all seams of the pouf, starting at the octagon. Separate six-ply embroidery floss into two-ply pieces and work with 18 inches of floss or less at one time. At the top of one seam, push up through the fabric at the edge of the octagon shape about ½ inch from the vertical seam.

Move your needle down ½ inch and over other side of seam. Push needle into the fabric about ¼ inch from seam and up another ¼ inch to right. Wrap thread under needle (M).

2. Draw the thread over the loop made with the last stitch (N).

3. Gently pull the thread taut to the right of the stitch (O).

4. Gently pull the thread taut at an angle across to the left side of the seam. Start your next stitch on the left, ½ inch lower than the stitch on the right and about 1 inch below the stitch directly above it on the same side (P).

5. Push the needle down through the fabric on the left side ¼ inch from the seam and up ½ inch from the seam with the thread under the needle.

Draw the thread over the loop and gently pull it taut to the left. Cross over to the right side again and continue down the seam. Repeat the stitching on each seam. Once all the sides are stitched, use the same decorative stitch around the edge of the top and bottom octagons (Q).

6. When all sides of each octagon are complete, remove the basting stitches from top and bottom pieces to finish (R).

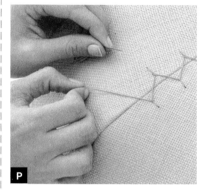
P

L

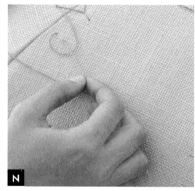
N

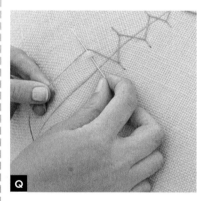
Q

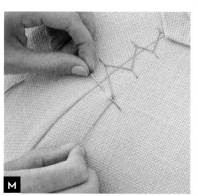
M

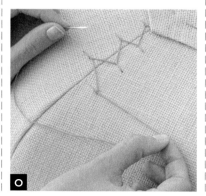
O

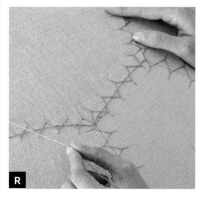
R

017
patch together a shower curtain

Brighten your morning routine by piecing blocks of fabrics and adding an easy, bold border to create a shower curtain.

YOU WILL NEED

6—⅔-yard pieces assorted pink prints and green prints (blocks)

2½ yards pink floral (border)

4⅛ yards solid white (lining)

2×72-inch strip heavyweight fusible interfacing

Embroidery floss: cream

Chalk

25—½ inch-diameter buttons

Plastic shower curtain liner

Shower curtain rings or hooks

Finished Shower Curtain:
72-inch square

Quantities are for 44/45-inch-wide, 100% cotton fabrics. All measurements include a ¼-inch seam allowance. Sew with right sides together unless otherwise stated.

CUT THE PIECES

To make the best use of your fabrics, cut pieces in the following order. Cut pink floral header and border strips and solid white lining rectangles lengthwise (parallel to the selvage). **Note:** Because the shower curtain will be laundered, be sure to prewash your fabrics.

From each assorted pink print and green print, cut:
36—10½ inch squares

From pink floral, cut:
2—6½×74¼-inch border strips
1—4½×72½-inch header strip
1—10¼×60½-inch border strip
1—4½×60½ -inch border strip

From solid white, cut:
1—36½×73¼-inch rectangle
2—18½×73¼-inch rectangles

ASSEMBLE SHOWER CURTAIN FRONT

1. Lay out 36 assorted print 10½-inch squares in six horizontal rows.

2. Sew together squares in each row. Press seams in one direction, alternating direction with each row. Join rows to make shower curtain center. Press seams in one direction. The shower curtain center should be 60½-inch square including seam allowances.

3. Join the pink floral 10¼×60½-inch border strip to bottom edge of shower curtain center. Join the pink floral 4½×60½-inch border strip to top edge of shower curtain center. Press seams toward border.

4. Sew a pink floral 6½×74¼-inch border strip to each remaining edge of curtain center to make curtain front. Press seams toward border.

5. Turn bottom edge of shower curtain front under 2 inches twice; sew along fold to complete shower curtain front.

ASSEMBLE AND ADD LINING

1. Join a solid white 18½×73¼-inch rectangle to each long edge of the solid white 36½×73¼-inch rectangle to make the lining. Press seams

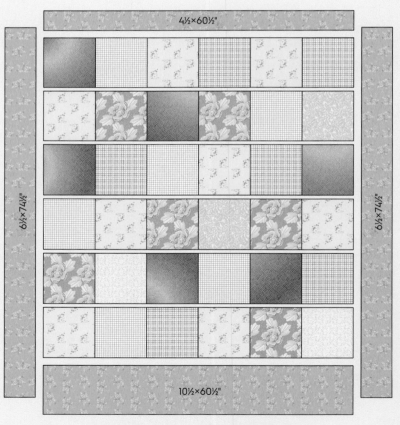

SHOWER CURTAIN ASSEMBLY DIAGRAM

mix & match

We mixed pastels and citrus-hued fabrics to come up with perky blocks for this uncomplicated, easy-to-piece shower curtain. We also added a full cotton lining and buttonholes for attaching the hooks. For a scrappy look, try making the blocks out of fat quarters.

toward center. Turn bottom edge of lining under 2 inches twice; sew along fold to complete lining.

2. With right sides together and top edges aligned, sew together shower curtain front and lining along side edges. Turn to right side and topstitch side edges. Baste together top edges of shower curtain front and lining.

ADD HEADER

1. With wrong sides together, press pink floral 4½×72½-inch header strip in half lengthwise. Open up strip and press under ¼ inch along one long edge.

2. Following manufacturer's instructions, fuse 2×72-inch interfacing strip to wrong side of header strip with pressed-under edge.

3. Pin unpressed edge of header strip to top edge of shower curtain, extending header strip ¼ inch beyond each shower curtain edge. Sew together; press seam toward header.

4. Fold header strip on previous fold with right sides together and long edges aligned. Sew short ends of header with ¼-inch seam allowance (even with finished side edges of shower curtain). Turn header right side out and whipstitch folded edge to inside of shower curtain.

FINISH SHOWER CURTAIN

1. With chalk, mark positions for buttonholes across pink floral header, using holes in plastic shower curtain liner as a guide for spacing. Following your sewing machine's instructions for making buttonholes, stitch a 1-inch vertical buttonhole at each mark.

2. Using six strands of embroidery floss, sew a button at each intersection of the pieced 10½-inch squares, catching the lining in the stitches.

3. To hang, insert shower curtain rings or hooks through holes in header and shower curtain liner.

SEWING TIPS

· Use a ¼-inch seam guide.

· Press or pin pieces together before sewing, but don't sew over the pins.

· Sew blocks and rows together without cutting threads between them (also know as chain-piecing).

· Clip threads as you go, so you don't have to work around extra threads.

· Organize your sewing. Have pieces ready to sew, extra bobbins wound, and your iron on and close by.

018
set a whimsical table

Adorable fabric pairs with hand-drawn scallops for a sweet, yet sophisticated table top design.

YOU WILL NEED

⅓ yard of cream novelty print

¾ yard of cream linen

20-inch length of black pom-pom fringe

Fabric markers: light green, dark green, black

Finished Table Mat: 19×26½ inches

Measurements include ½-inch seam allowances. Sew with right sides together unless otherwise stated.

CUT THE PIECES

From cream linen, cut:

1—19¾×20-inch rectangle

From cream novelty print, fussy-cut:

1—8¾×20-inch strip

1. Sew cream linen 19¾×20-inch rectangle and cream novelty print 8¾×20-inch strip together to make the table mat (Diagram 1).

2. Turn under ¼ inch along each long edge of table mat; press. Turn under ¼ inch again; press. Sew through all layers close to first folded edge (Diagram 2). Repeat along top short edge of table mat.

3. Turn under ¼ inch along bottom short edge of table mat; press. Turn under ¼ inch again; press. Pin pom-pom trim to wrong side of bottom edge of table mat, positioning it so the pom-poms extend below the pressed edge. Sew through all layers.

4. Using fabric markers and referring to photo, draw scalloped lines onto lower half of the linen portion of table mat.

DIAGRAM 1

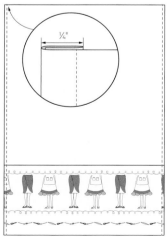

DIAGRAM 2

O19
tie on an apron

The piecing on this kitchen-inspired apron is easy peasy! Simply join four fabric strips to make the body and add a cream novelty print lining to the back.

YOU WILL NEED

4—¾-yard pieces of assorted prints in coral, big dot, small green dot, and cream novelty (apron, pocket, lining)

1 yard green rickrack

2—1½-yard pieces of ⅞-inch-wide grosgrain ribbon: cream and green

Water-soluble marking pen

Finished Apron: 21×28½ inches (overall); 21×22½ inches (folded)

Quantities are for 44/45-inches-wide, 100% cotton fabrics. Measurements include ¼-inch seam allowances unless otherwise indicated. Sew with right sides together unless otherwise indicated.

CUT THE PIECES

From coral print, cut:
2—5¾×30-inch strips

From big dot, cut:
2—5¾×30-inch strips

From small green dot, cut:
1—6¾×14-inch rectangle

From cream novelty print, cut:
1—21½×30-inch rectangle

From green rickrack, cut:
1—22-inch-long piece
1—7-inch-long piece

1. Sew together two coral print 5¾×30-inch strips and two big dot 5¾×30-inch strips to make apron front (Diagram 1). Press seams in one direction. Apron front should be 21½×30 inches including seam allowances.

2. Topstitch along one side of each seam (Diagram 2).

3. Layer cream novelty print 21½×30-inch rectangle and apron front with right sides together, orienting the prints in opposite directions so that the cream novelty print rectangle is right side up when the top is folded over the front. Sew together around all edges, leaving a 4-inch opening

along one edge for turning. Trim diagonally across corners.

4. Turn right side out through opening. Press flat and slip-stitch opening closed. The apron unit should be 21×29½ inches.

5. Topstitch along outer edge of the apron unit and remaining side of each seam (Diagram 3).

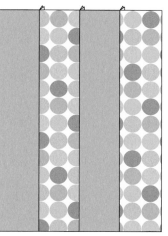

DIAGRAM 1

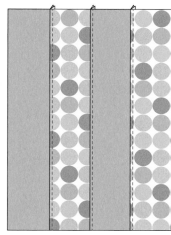

DIAGRAM 2

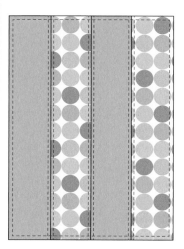

DIAGRAM 3

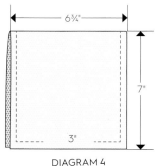

DIAGRAM 4

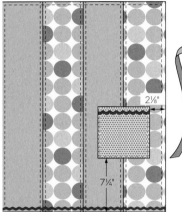

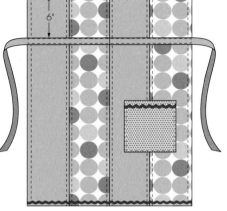

DIAGRAM 5

DIAGRAM 6

6. Turn under bottom edge of apron unit ½ inch; press. Turn under again ½ inch; press. Sew through all layers close to first folded edge to hem apron unit.

7. Referring to photo on previous page, pin 22-inch-long piece of green rickrack over hem stitching, folding ends over edges. Using contrasting thread, stitch through center of rickrack.

8. Aligning short edges, fold small green dot 6¾×14-inch rectangle in half, right side inside, to make a 6¾×7-inch rectangle. Sew together raw edges, leaving a 3-inch opening along one edge for turning (Diagram 4).

9. Turn right side out through opening. Press flat and slip-stitch opening closed to make a pocket.

10. Referring to photo on previous page, pin 7-inch-long piece of green rickrack 1 inch from folded

edge of pocket, folding ends over edges. Using contrasting thread, stitch to pocket through center of rickrack.

11. Position pocket on right side of apron unit 7¼ inches from bottom edge and 2⅛ inches from right-hand edge; pin. Topstitch side and bottom edges of pocket to make apron body (Diagram 5).

12. Join ends of cream and green grosgrain ribbon pieces to make a tie strip. Press seam open.

13. Using a water-soluble marking pen, draw a line on right side of apron body 6 inches from top edge. Align and center top edge of tie strip with marked line; pin. Topstitch tie to apron body along both edges of ribbon to complete apron (Diagram 6). To wear apron, tie ribbon ends around waist. Fold top of apron lining over ribbon tie strip as shown in photo.

020
personalize your pot holders

Make your own heat-safe hot pads using batting and pretty fabrics.

YOU WILL NEED
9×11-inch rectangle green dot (pot holder border and hanging loop)
9×11-inch rectangle novelty print (pot holder center)
8-inch square backing fabric
7½-inch square insulated batting
8-inch square cotton batting
Quilt basting spray
Chopstick (optional)

Finished Pot Holder: 7½-inch square

Quantities are for 100% cotton fabrics. Measurements include ¼-inch seam allowances unless otherwise indicated. Sew with right sides together unless otherwise indicated.

DIAGRAM 1

DIAGRAM 2

DIAGRAM 3

DIAGRAM 4

CUT THE PIECES

From green dot, cut:
2—1½×8-inch border strips
2—1½×6-inch border strips
1—2×5-inch strip

From novelty print, fussy-cut:
1—6-inch square

1. Sew short green dot border strips to opposite edges of novelty print 6-inch square (Diagram 1). Join long green dot border strips to remaining edges to make pot holder front. Press all seams toward green dot strips. The pot holder front should be 8-inch square including seam allowances.

2. With wrong side inside, fold green dot 2×5-inch strip in half lengthwise (Diagram 2). Lightly press, then unfold. Fold long raw edges in to meet at center. Fold at center to hide raw edges, aligning folded edges; press again. Edgestitch double-folded edge. Matching raw ends, fold in half to make a loop; baste.

3. With raw ends to outside, pin loop to top left-hand corner of pot holder front (Diagram 3).

4. Apply basting spray to one side of insulated batting square and cotton batting square.

5. Place insulated batting square, basting spray side up, on a flat surface. Center and top with cotton batting square, basting spray side up. Layer pot holder front, right side up, and backing square, wrong side up, on batting squares to make layered unit. Stitch through all layers around outer edges, pivoting at corners and leaving a 5-inch opening along one edge (Diagram 4). Trim.

6. Turn layered unit right side out. Using a chopstick or the eraser end of a pencil, push out corners. Whipstitch opening closed.

021
pretty up an oven mitt

Protect your hands with a project that doubles as darling decor.

YOU WILL NEED

½ yard muslin (lining)

½ yard novelty print (oven mitt)

⅛ yard green dot (binding, hanging loop)

18-inch square cotton batting

18-inch square insulated batting, such as Insul-Bright

Quilt basting spray

Finished Oven Mitt: 8×13 inches

Quantities are for 44/45-inch-wide, 100% cotton fabrics. Measurements include ¼-inch seam allowances unless otherwise indicated. Sew with right sides together unless otherwise indicated.

1. Trace patterns on next page onto white paper; enlarge and cut out. Cut the pieces in the following order:

From muslin, cut:
1 each of Patterns A and A reversed

From novelty print, cut:
1 each of Patterns A and A reversed

From green dot, cut:
1—2¾×20-inch binding strip
1—2×5-inch strip

From cotton batting, cut:
2 of Pattern A

From insulated batting, cut:
2 of Pattern B

2. Following manufacturer's instructions, apply basting spray to wrong side of muslin A reversed piece. Lay out a cotton batting A piece and an insulated batting B piece with thumb of each piece facing same direction as muslin piece; apply basting spray to batting.

3. Place muslin A reversed piece wrong side up on a flat surface. Top with cotton batting A piece, basting spray side up. Center and top with insulated batting B piece, basting spray side up. Top with novelty print A piece, right side up, aligning edges with layered A pieces (Diagram 1, next page).

4. Quilt layered pieces as desired to make front. The featured oven mitt is quilted in a 1½-inch diagonal grid.

5. Repeat Steps 2 and 3 with muslin A

piece, remaining cotton batting A piece and insulated batting B piece, and novelty print A reversed piece to make mitt back.

6. With wrong side inside, fold green dot 2¾×20-inch binding strip in half lengthwise; press. Cut strip into two 10-inch-long binding pieces.

7. Aligning raw edges, sew one binding piece to upper edge of mitt front (Diagram 2). Fold binding to lining side. Stitch in the ditch or hand-sew binding to lining (see #094).

8. Repeat Step 7 with mitt back and remaining red dot binding piece.

9. Using green dot 2×5-inch strip, repeat Step 3 of Pot Holder, previous page, to make a loop.

10. Pin raw ends of loop to side edge of mitt front next to binding (Diagram 3).

11. Layer mitt front and mitt back with right sides together. Beginning at one bound upper edge, sew together through all layers (Diagram 4). Stitch again ⅛ inch from outer edges. Clip into seam allowance along curves just up to outer line of stitching; zigzag or serge seams.

13. Turn right side out and press to complete oven mitt.

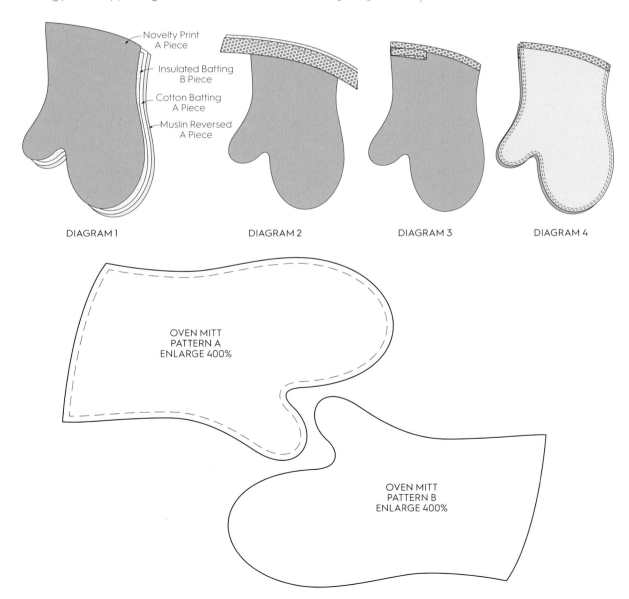

Novelty Print A Piece
Insulated Batting B Piece
Cotton Batting A Piece
Muslin Reversed A Piece

DIAGRAM 1   DIAGRAM 2   DIAGRAM 3   DIAGRAM 4

OVEN MITT PATTERN A ENLARGE 400%

OVEN MITT PATTERN B ENLARGE 400%

—Make in Minutes—

Perk up a table with a favorite color or pattern with these super quick place mats you can make with supplies pulled from your fabric stash.

022
set the table

YOU WILL NEED

For two place mats:

½ yard each of four assorted light yellow prints

2—13×18-inch rectangles heavy interfacing

Quilt-basting spray

Finished Place Mat: 13×18 inches

Quantities are for 44/45-inch-wide, 100% cotton fabrics. Measurements include ¼-inch seam allowances unless otherwise indicated. Sew with right sides together unless otherwise indicated.

If binding your place mats with a directional fabric, cut two binding strips on lengthwise grain of fabric and two binding strips on widthwise grain. Miter the corners of the binding so the fabric lines or motifs all run in the same direction.

Patterns are on Pattern Page Q.

CUT THE PIECES

From light yellow print 1, cut:
4 of Pattern A

From light yellow print 2, cut:
4 of Pattern B

From light yellow print 3, cut:
2—13×18-inch rectangles

From light yellow print 4, cut:
4—4½×42-inch binding strips

ASSEMBLE PLACE MATS

1. For one place mat you will need two each of light yellow prints A and

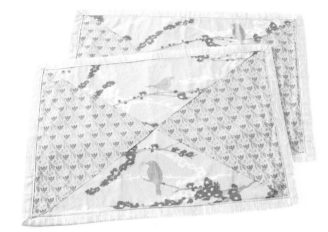

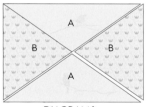

DIAGRAM 1

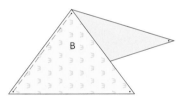

DIAGRAM 2

B triangles, one 13×18-inch rectangle, and two 4×42-inch binding strips. Lay out A and B triangles in a rectangle.

2. Sew together A and B triangles to make a large triangle. Press seam toward A piece.

3. Repeat Step 2 with remaining A and B triangles.

4. Join large triangles to make place mat top. Press seam.

5. Place light yellow print 13×18-inch rectangle, wrong side up, on paper-covered flat surface. Lightly spray rectangle with quilt-basting spray. Aligning edges, center 13×18-inch interfacing rectangle on adhesive-sprayed light yellow print

rectangle. Lightly spray interfacing rectangle with quilt-basting spray. Aligning edges, center place mat top, right side up, on adhesive-sprayed interfacing rectangle. Baste layers together around the place mat ⅜ inch from the edges.

6. Repeat Steps 2 through 5 for a second place mat.

BIND PLACE MATS

1. Join two light yellow print 4½×42-inch binding strips for each place mat.

2. Using a ¾-inch-wide seam allowance, bind mat with binding strips. (For details, see #094.) Topstitch binding ⅛ inch from inner edges.

023
quilt modern pot holders

Use heat-resistant insulated batting and cotton batting for these scrappy hot pads or pot holders. For more details on quilting techniques, see #093.

YOU WILL NEED

For two hot pads:

23—5-inch squares or ¾ yard total assorted florals, prints, and stripes in blue, tan, yellow, coral, cream, green, and aqua (front and back units)

½ yard solid cream (binding)

⅝ yard muslin (backing)

24-inch square each of cotton batting and insulated batting, such as Insul-Bright

Finished Pot Holder:

10½ inches square

Yardages and cutting instructions are based on 42 inches of usable fabric width. Measurements include ¼-inch seam allowances unless otherwise indicated. Sew with right sides together unless otherwise indicated.

CUT THE PIECES

From each assorted floral, print, or stripe 5 inch square, cut:

4—2½-inch squares (you will use 90 of the 92 total squares cut)

From solid cream, cut:

Enough 2½-inch-wide bias strips to total 120 inches in length, cutting and piecing to make 2—2½×44-inch and 2—2½×10½-inch binding strips (For details, see #098.)

From muslin, cut:

2—11-inch squares

2—9×11-inch rectangles

From each cotton and insulated batting, cut:

2—11-inch squares

2—9×11-inch rectangles

1. Lay out 20 assorted floral, print, and stripe 2½-inch squares in four horizontal rows (Diagram 1). Sew together squares in each row. Press seams open. Join rows to make a front unit. Press seams open. The front unit should be 10½×8½ inches including seam allowances.

2. Center front unit right side up atop one each of insulated batting, cotton batting, and muslin 9×11-inch rectangles; baste.

3. Quilt as desired.

4. Trim battings and muslin even with front unit to make a quilted pocket rectangle. The pocket rectangle should be 10½×8½ inches including seam allowances.

5. Using Corner Cutting Pattern on Pattern Page A mark cutting line at each corner of one long edge of quilted pocket rectangle for rounding corners (Diagram 2).

Machine-baste a scant ⅛ inch inside lines. Trim along drawn lines. Machine-baste remaining edges.

6. Using one solid cream 2½×10½-inch bias strip, bind long straight edge of pocket rectangle.

7. Lay out 25 assorted floral, print, and stripe 2½-inch squares in five rows (Diagram 3). Sew together squares in each row. Press seams open. Join rows to make a back unit. Press seams open. The back unit should be 10½-inch square including seam allowances.

8. Center back unit right side up atop one each of insulated batting, cotton batting, and muslin 11-inch squares; baste as before.

9. Quilt as desired.

10. Trim battings and muslin even with back unit to make a quilted back piece. The back piece should be a 10½-inch square including seam allowances. Using Corner Cutting Pattern on Pattern Page A and referring to Step 5, mark, baste, and trim all corners on back piece. Machine-baste remaining edges.

11. With right sides facing up, layer pocket rectangle atop back piece. Sew together using ⅛-inch seam (Diagram 4).

12. Using a solid cream 2½×44-inch bias strip, bind outer edges to complete one pot holder.

13. Repeat Steps 1 through 12 to make a second pot holder if desired.

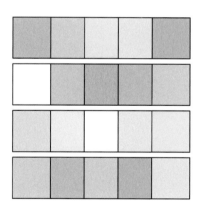

DIAGRAM 1

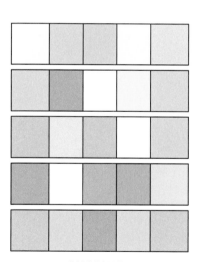

DIAGRAM 3

DIAGRAM 4

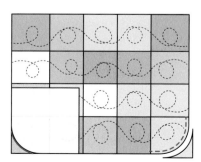

DIAGRAM 2

Simple Storage Solutions

Keep your supplies contained—whether they're in the living room, kitchen, or crafts room—with bags, bins, and baskets you can whip up in no time at all.

024
make a case for baskets

Whip up a handled bag like the one on the previous pages by stitching together some sweater-wrapped clothesline.

YOU WILL NEED

Approximately 100 feet of ¼-inch-wide clothesline

Old sweaters: various shades of gray, various bright colors

Sewing thread: gray

Finished Bag: 8 inches tall×17 inches wide (with handles)

1. Cut old sweaters into 1¼-inch-wide strips, cutting each as long as possible. Wrap a dark gray strip clockwise around the clothesline, overlapping the strip as you go.

2. Fold the first 10 inches of covered clothesline over on itself in a U-shape. Referring to How To Sew a Cord Coil, below (making an oval instead of a circle), and using gray thread, sew between the clothesline rows along the 10-inch length to begin the bag bottom. Continue adding gray sweater strips and coiling the clothesline to make an approximately 3×11-inch oval coil for the bag bottom. Do not trim clothesline.

3. To begin the bag sides, lay the wrapped clothesline over the top of the outermost row of oval coil. Shift the base under the sewing machine foot so the oval is flipped up slightly on the left side of the foot. Continue sewing between the rows, adding sweater strip wraps and coiling the clothesline on top of the base.

4. Where desired, add strips of light gray to make horizontal rows around bag sides. Add random, brightly colored short strips as desired.

5. When the bag sides reach approximately 7-inches tall, add a handle to one wide side by leaving a 7-inch-long portion of the covered cording unstitched. Shape the handle as desired, leaving a gap between the coil and the handle. Backstitch at the beginning and end of the handle where it attaches to the coil for extra reinforcement.

6. Continue sewing the coil until you reach the opposite side. Repeat Step 5 to add a handle opposite the first handle.

7. Continue sewing one more complete round around bag sides, adding a second layer to each handle.

8. Trim cord to end along the top of a bag side near the base of a handle. Wrap a sweater strip onto the cord, extending the wraps past the end of the cord by 1 inch; trim strip if necessary. Finish sewing the covered cord to the coil, reinforcing at the end with backstitches.

HOW TO SEW A CORD COIL

1. For a round base, coil one end of the cord tightly around itself a few times until the coil is the size of a quarter.

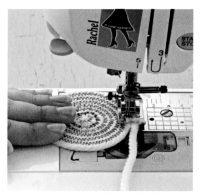

2. While holding coil firmly, place the coil under your sewing machine's zigzag foot with the cord extending off the right side toward you. Use a wide zigzag to stitch between the cording rows, catching the cording on both sides to hold it together.

3. Slowly rotate the coils counterclockwise as you zigzag-stitch in between the rows. For long continuous curves, you may wish to switch to an open-toe sewing machine foot. Tilt coil as you stitch to build sides.

025
sew a place for specs

Set your sights on a handy eyeglass case stitched from hand-dyed cord. The shade variations along the length of the cord create subtle striping on the caddy sides.

YOU WILL NEED

Rit Liquid Dye: Evening Blue, Denim Blue

Paper cup

Bucket

Approximately 25 feet of ³⁄₁₆-inch cord

Wooden dowel that is long enough to extend over bucket

Artist's paintbrush

Sewing thread: monofilament

1-inch-diameter decorative button

Clear-drying crafts glue

Finished Eyeglass Case: *4×7 inches*

DYE THE CORD

1. Place a few drops of Denim Blue liquid dye in a paper cup; set aside. Mix Evening Blue with 1 gallon of hot water in a bucket.

2. Wrap cord around your arm to make large loops; tie ends together. Wet the rope under a faucet to make the rope drape evenly.

3. Dip the cord loops about three-fourths of the way into the bucket of dye; soak for 5 minutes. **Note:** Lay a dowel over the bucket and drape top of cord over the dowel during soak time.

4. Remove cord. Add a full bottle of Denim Blue into dye bath. Dip the cord loops back into dye, about halfway in; soak for up to 5 minutes.

5. Pull cord up, leaving one-fourth of rope submerged in dye; soak for 1 hour.

6. Remove cord from dye. Brush dye from paper cup onto cord where you want for more contrast. Let dry.

ASSEMBLE THE EYEGLASS CASE

1. Fold the first 5 inches of dyed cord over on itself to form a thin U-shape. Referring to How To Sew a Cord Coil, opposite (making an oval instead of a circle), and using clear thread, sew between the two clothesline rows. Continue coiling around the first row, so that the starting end of the clothesline is secure. Continue to stitch four rounds to finish stitching the base.

2. To begin the case sides, lay the cord over the top of the outermost row of the base coil. Shift the base under the sewing machine foot so the coil is flipped up vertically on the left side of the foot. Continue sewing between the rounds until the case sides are 4 inches tall.

3. To make a closure, form a 1¼-inch loop along the center of one side and trim cord end. Make sure loop is large enough to accommodate button; stitch in place. Zigzag-stitch the bottom of the loop to the top edge of case side.

4. Hand-stitch a button to outside top edge of opposite case side aligned with the loop. Slip loop over button to close the case.

026
create a catchall

Turn your chaos into productive spaces with coordinating catchalls made from embroidery hoops. Crisscross ribbons allow for tucking and pinning pictures and receipts.

YOU WILL NEED

10-inch-diameter wooden embroidery hoop
Fat quarter (18×22 inches) of fabric
45-inch length of ⅛-inch-wide grosgrain ribbon
Hand-sewing needle
Sewing thread to match ribbon
Tacky glue
2-inch-tall wooden clothespins

1. Remove inner ring from embroidery hoop. Lay fabric right side up over the inner ring, positioning the portion of fabric you wish to frame. Put embroidery hoop back together, pushing fabric between the pieces to hold it in place. Tighten the screw and adjust fabric tension as needed.

2. Lay grosgrain ribbon in a zigzag pattern across the framed fabric; place a pin where ribbon changes direction at each end. Trim ribbon ends if necessary.

3. Secure ribbon to the fabric with a few small stitches using doubled sewing thread and a sewing needle; remove pins.

4. Turn hoop over and trim fabrics.

5. Run a line of tacky glue along inner ring back edge; press fabric edges into glue to prevent fraying; let dry.

6. Pin clothespins to ribbon.

027
circle round a wall pocket

Mix and match your favorite patterned fabrics and whip up fun and functional organizers that feature pockets for pens, pencils, and letters.

YOU WILL NEED

10-inch-diameter wooden embroidery hoop
2 fat quarters (18×22 inches each) of coordinating fabrics
Tacky glue

1. Fold fabric for pocket in half with wrong sides together to measure 18×11 inches Using a straight stitch on the sewing machine, topstitch a scant ⅛ inch from the folded edge along its length. Topstitch a second straight line approximately ⅜ inch below the first topstitched line (Diagram 1, next page). This is the top pocket edge.

2. Fold pocket in half to measure 9×11 inches; finger-press or use an iron to crease. Unfold pocket; lay on top of background fabric, aligning bottom and side edges (Diagram 2, next page).

3. Topstitch a straight vertical seam along pocket crease line, creating a divider and joining to background fabric (Diagram 3).

4. Follow Step 1 of #026, previous page, to insert fabric into embroidery hoop. Follow Steps 4 and 5 to finish the back.

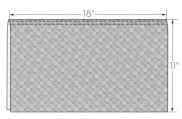

18"

11"

DIAGRAM 1

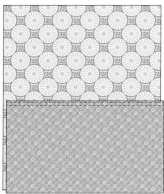

DIAGRAM 2

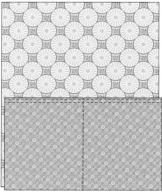

DIAGRAM 3

028
max out wall storage

Felt loops keep keys at the ready and always easy to find.

YOU WILL NEED

14½-inch-diameter wooden embroidery hoop

3 fat quarters (18×22 inches each) of coordinating fabrics (background, pocket 1, pocket 2)

Ruler

Air-soluble marking pen

Computer and printer

¾-inch-wide iron-on veneer

½×16-inch felt strip

1¼-inch-diameter hinged metal rings

Tacky glue

1. Fold background fabric in half with wrong sides together to measure 9×22 inches; press.

2. Fold pocket 1 and pocket 2 fabrics in half with wrong sides together to measure 11×18 inches each; press.

3. Place pocket 2 on top of pocket 3 with pressed edges at top and aligning all edges. Measure 7 inches from left of top right-hand corner; mark. Measure 7 inches down from top right-hand corner; mark. Using a ruler and air-soluble marking pen, connect the marks to form a diagonal line (Diagram 1, opposite).

4. Using a straight stitch, stitch along the drawn line. Trim off the corner ½ inch beyond stitched line (Diagram 2, opposite). Press the seam allowances open.

5. Open pocket panel and press (Diagram 3, opposite).

6. Use computer and printer to choose a typeface and print words "In" and "Out" onto paper in the size

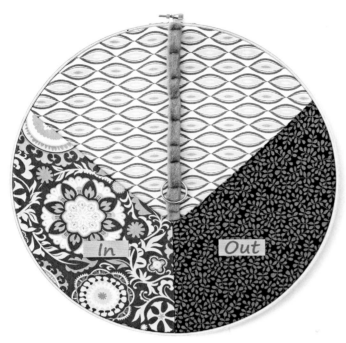

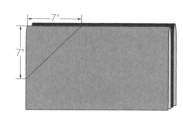

DIAGRAM 1

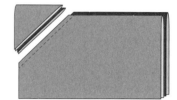

DIAGRAM 2

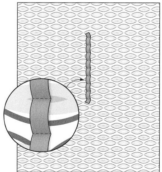

DIAGRAM 3

you want (use a font size that produces letters less than ¾ inch tall). Cut a piece of iron-on veneer to fit each word. Apply temporary adhesive to back of veneer pieces and attach over each word on printed samples. Feed paper back through printer to print words on veneer.

7. Remove adhesive from each piece of veneer. Following manufacturer's instructions, use an iron to attach a veneer word to each pocket.

8. Unfold background fabric so the crease is vertical. Measure 4 inches down from the top along vertical crease; mark. Measure 1 inch down from first mark, staying on the vertical crease; mark. Continue marking until you have a total of nine marks.

9. Place the felt strip along the vertical crease. Topstitch the piece to

background fabric at each mark with a short horizontal seam, leaving a short raised half loop between each seam (Diagram 4). **Note:** Insert your index finger under the felt strip as a guideline to determine how high each raised portion should be.

10. Place the pocket panel on top of the background fabric, aligning the pocket divider seam with the vertical crease on the fabric, just below the felt loop line. Sew in the ditch of the divider pocket line to secure the pocket to the background fabric.

11. Follow Step 1 of #026 to insert fabric into embroidery hoop. Follow Steps 4 and 5 to finish the back.

12. Attach hinged rings to felt loops with tacky glue.

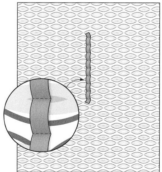

DIAGRAM 4

029
pick a berry basket bin

Inspired by berry baskets from the farmers market, these cheery fabric renditions are great for stashing notions in a crafts room, corralling change, or holding jewelry. Take your pick from a small or a large version.

YOU WILL NEED

- 2—12-inch pieces of two coordinating fabrics (small basket)
- 2—18-inch squares of two coordinating fabrics (large basket)
- ¼ yard of double-sided fusible heavyweight interface (such as 72F Peltex II)
- 1 yard of ½-inch double-fold binding tape
- Clothespins

Finished Baskets: 4¼×4¼×1½ inches (small); 5×5×3½ inches (large)

Measurements include ¼-inch seam allowances unless otherwise indicated. Sew with right sides together unless otherwise indicated.

Enlarge and cut out patterns on Pattern Page D. For a small basket, fold fabric in half. For a large basket, fold fabric in quarters. Cut the following pieces:

FOR ONE SMALL BASKET

From print 1, cut:
1 of Pattern A (exterior)

From print 2, cut:
1 of Pattern A (interior)

From double-sided fusible heavyweight interfacing, cut:
1—3¾-inch square (bottom)
4—3¾×1¼-inch rectangles (sides)

FOR ONE LARGE BASKET

From print 3, cut:
1 of Pattern B (exterior)

From print 4, cut:
1 of Pattern B (interior)

From double-sided fusible heavyweight interfacing, cut:
1—4¾-inch square (bottom)
4—4¾×3¼-inch rectangles (sides)

1. Place matching exterior and lining pieces with right sides together; sew pieces together at each corner as shown by lines on Diagram 1.

DIAGRAM 1

DIAGRAM 2

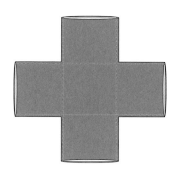

DIAGRAM 3

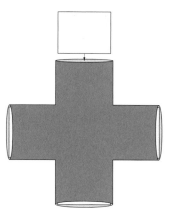

DIAGRAM 4

2. Place corresponding interfacing square on center of exterior side of shape; press (Diagram 2). Clip into corners slightly and turn right side out.

3. Slip one corresponding interfacing rectangle into top, bottom, and each side of shape (Diagram 3). Adjust shapes so there is enough space around interfacing edges to allow for topstitching. Press shape on both sides.

4. Topstitch around center and side interfacing pieces (Diagram 4). Place

shape with exterior side down.

5. Open double-fold binding tape. Fold one side of box up. Turn end of bias tape under ½ inch and place end of tape in center of box side, aligning tape and box side edges; pin (Diagram 5).

6. Working around box and leaving a ½-inch gap of unpinned bias tape at each corner, pin bias tape in same manner to all sides. Overlap ends of tape by at least 1 inch. Sew ½ inch

below top edge of each side panel and corner (Diagram 6).

7. Flip binding tape up and over the top of the basket to conceal raw side edges. Fold inside of binding under ½ inch and hold tape in place using clothespins. Working on outside of basket, topstitch binding a scant ⅛ inch above bottom of binding, catching inside of binding in seam (Diagram 7).

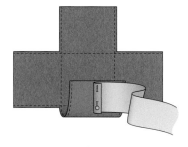

DIAGRAM 5

DIAGRAM 6

DIAGRAM 7

030
stash supplies in style

Hang these wide-mouth bags anywhere you need a place to quickly stash bits and pieces or often-used items. A wooden embroidery hoop keeps each bag open. Hooks on the backs make them easy to suspend from a rod.

YOU WILL NEED

⅓ yard multicolor print (outer bag)

⅓ yard complementary tone-on-tone (bag lining)

6-inch-diameter embroidery hoop with screw assembly

S-hook

Curtain rod (optional)

Drapery ring (optional)

Finished Bag: 6½×8×3 inches

Measurements include ½-inch seam allowances unless otherwise indicated. Sew with right sides together unless otherwise indicated.

CUT THE PIECES

From multicolor print, cut:

2—10½-inch squares

From tone-on-tone, cut:

2—10½-inch squares

1. Sew together multicolor print 10½-inch squares along three edges to make outer bag (Diagram 1). Press seams to one side or open.

2. At one sewn corner of outer bag, match seams to create a flattened triangle (Diagram 2). Measuring 1½ inches from point of triangle, draw a 3-inch-long line across triangle. Sew on drawn line. Trim excess fabric, leaving ½-inch seam allowance. Repeat at remaining sewn corner to shape bottom of

outer bag. Turn the outer bag right side out.

3. Using tone-on-tone 10½-inch squares instead of multicolor print squares, repeat Step 1, leaving a 3-inch opening in center of one edge, to make bag lining.

4. Repeat Step 2 to shape bottom of bag lining. Leave lining wrong side out.

5. Insert outer bag into bag lining and align raw edges (Diagram 3). Sew together raw edges. Turn right side out through opening in lining. Slipstitch opening closed. Insert lining into outer bag and press top edge flat. Topstitch close to top edge to complete bag.

6. Separate inner and outer embroidery hoops. Place inner hoop around top of bag 1 to 2 inches from bag upper edge. Fold bag upper edge over inner hoop so lining shows (bag will be snug around hoop). Place outer hoop around inner hoop with screw assembly centered in back; tighten.

7. Hook screw assembly over an S-hook. If you're using a large S-hook, hang hook directly from curtain rod. If you're using a small S-hook, hook it into the hole of a drapery ring, then hang the drapery ring from a curtain rod.

DIAGRAM 1

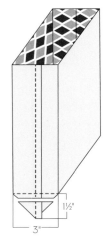

DIAGRAM 2

DIAGRAM 3

031
green up your lunch

Ditch plastic bags forever with this fun (and washable) sandwich wrap.

YOU WILL NEED

Outer fabric, 14½-inch square (see Food & Fabric, opposite)

Lining fabric, 12½-inch square (see Food & Fabric, opposite)

Ruler

Polyester thread

Fabric pen (optional)

Ribbon, ⅞ inch wide (optional)

T-shirt transfer paper (optional)

Small amount of fabric glue (optional)

Bobby pins

Sew-on Velcro, ¾×4½ inches (Cut the hard, hook side to 1½ inches. Leave the soft, loop side at 4½ inches.)

1. With wrong side of outer fabric up, fold in a ½-inch seam on one side and press. Fold in a ½-inch seam again and press to finish seam. Repeat on other three sides.

2. Miter corners either by simply folding or sewing.

3. If you are attaching a label, do so now. Write name on ribbon or use T-shirt transfer paper, following manufacturer's directions. Measure the desired length of the label, and add ¼ to ½ inch on each side for folding over. (We measured ¾ inch from the edge of the letters.)

Fold behind on ends and finger-press. Use a small amount of fabric glue to hold in place if desired.

Place fabric, right side up, in front of you, as a diamond. Select which corner is going to be your top flap. Put that corner at the bottom.

Center the label 2½ inches up

from the bottom corner. Sew into place using matching or contrasting thread; press.

4. Place outer fabric, right side down, on table. Place liner fabric, right side up (on PUL, this is the slick, shiny side), on top. Tuck liner under the unsewn seams of the outer fabric. Trim liner if needed so it fits flat. Use bobby pins to hold liner in place if needed.

5. Using ⅛-inch seam allowance, sew down inner edge of folded seam.

6. Choose a corner to be the top flap, or find the corner used for label. Sew the 1½-inch Velcro ½ inch down from the corner, on the liner fabric, using a ⅛-inch seam allowance.

7. Sew the 4½-inch loop tape ½ inch down from the opposite corner, on the outer fabric, using a ⅛-inch seam allowance.

032
pack superior snacks

Eat well on the go with reusable snack bags you can easily wash.

YOU WILL NEED

(Measurements for smaller bag are in parentheses.)

Two pieces of outer fabric, each 8¾×7¼ inches (6¾×6¼ inches) (If using stripes or a directional pattern, the longer measurement is the width of the finished piece. The shorter measurement is the height.)

Two pieces of lining fabric, each 8¾×7¼ inches (6¾×6¼ inches)

Polyester thread

Ruler

Bobby pins

Chopstick (optional)

Strip of sew-on Velcro, approximately 7 inches long (approximately 5 inches)

All seam allowances are ¼ inch unless otherwise indicated.

1. Enlarge and cut out fabric pieces on Pattern Page A. With right sides together, sew one outer piece and one liner piece together along one of the long sides. This is one bag unit. Repeat with remaining two pieces.

2. Open two bag units and stack, right sides together, matching the fabrics (outer above outer, liner above liner). Use bobby pins to hold.

3. Sew along perimeter of the stacked units, leaving approximately 2 inches open on the outer fabric portion at the bottom. Make sure to lay the first joined seam flat, folding liner over liner and outer over outer to help the finished pouch lie flat.

4. If you want boxed corners, follow the next steps. If not, clip corners and skip to Step 5. Picking any corner, match bottom seam line to side seam line, creating a triangle. Measuring 1 inch in from the triangle point, draw a 2-inch-long line across the triangle. Sew along the drawn line. Trim excess fabric to a ¼-inch seam. Repeat with other corners.

5. Turn piece right side out through open seam. Use fingers or a chopstick to complete corner turns.

6. Tuck liner into bag and shape as needed. Finger-press the top edge where the two fabrics are joined.

7. Using bobby pins, center and hold the loop side of Velcro to one inner side of the top opening. Sew down with a ⅛-inch seam.

8. Using bobby pins, center and hold the hook side of Velcro to one of the inner sides of the top opening. Sew down with a ⅛-inch seam.

9. Sew bottom seam closed using a ladder stitch.

food & fabric

- For outer fabric, 100% cotton works best, but you can use anything you have.
- Sandwich wraps and snack pouches can be made using fabric quarters or 18×22-inch fat quarters for the outer fabric, which means inexpensive fabric and less leftover material. Allow extra fabric for prints such as diagonal stripes.
- Prewash all fabrics, especially if you are using a dark fabric that might bleed; press the fabric.
- Use polyester thread, which resists moisture transfer. This helps prevent food from drying out.
- For the liner, ripstop nylon can replace polyurethane laminate (PUL) and still offer moisture resistance, but it is harder to sew.
- Diaper precuts are the perfect size for the PUL. Again, less waste. But you are not likely to find a precut in white.
- Use bobby pins instead of regular pins. They hold just as well and don't leave holes that compromise the moisture resistance of the piece.

033
store jewels safely

A gift bag that's useful even after the gift is open? What a concept! This little elastic cinch bag is perfect for wrapping up jewelry, such as the pendants shown, and can later be clipped wherever you want to keep something safely stashed.

YOU WILL NEED

2—4½×5-inch rectangles of one print (outside)

Water-soluble marking pen

2—4½×5-inch rectangles of second print (lining)

6-inch length of ribbon

Metal key ring with clip

10-inch length of ¼-inch-wide cotton elastic

Sew with ¼-inch seam allowances and right sides together.

1. Using a water-soluble marking pen, mark ¾ inch and 1¼ inches below the top edge of one 4½×5-inch outside rectangle. If using a key ring that does not unclip, thread the hook portion of the key ring onto the ribbon. Fold the ribbon in half and pin the ribbon ends together just above bottom mark (Diagram 1).

2. Place the two 4½×5-inch outside rectangles together with right sides facing and the key ring between the layers. Sew the sides and bottom, catching the ribbon ends in the seam. Clip bottom corners (Diagram 2) and turn right side out.

3. Place the two 4½×5-inch lining rectangles together with right sides facing. Using a water-soluble marking pen, mark ¾ inch and 1¼ inches below the top edge. Sew the sides and bottom, leaving the

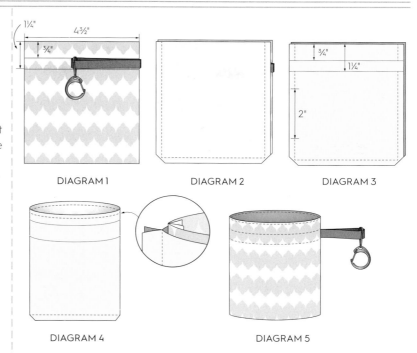

DIAGRAM 1   DIAGRAM 2   DIAGRAM 3

DIAGRAM 4   DIAGRAM 5

area between the marks unstitched and a 2-inch opening along one side. Clip bottom corners (Diagram 3).

4. Slip outside into lining with right sides together. Match seams; pin (Diagram 4).

5. Sew outside and lining together along the top edge. Turn right side out through opening; press.

6. Turn under the opening in the lining side and hand-sew it closed. Tuck the lining into the pouch and press. Topstitch around the top. Sew around the pouch on marked lines to make a casing (Diagram 5).

7. Insert elastic into hole in lining and feed through the casing. Holding elastic ends together at the seam opening, adjust the elastic so it is tight but still loose enough to open and close the top of the bag. Sew the elastic ends together and insert the stitched ends into the casing. Hand-stitch the opening closed.

Pincushions & Notions

Corral your sewing supplies in style and make cleaning up a breeze with these creative storage solutions.

034
do a doughnut pincushion

Topped with your choice of icing or sprinkles, these felt doughnuts are a guilt-free way to enjoy your favorite treat. Use embroidery stitches for appliquéing and embellishing each one and use beads for the sprinkles.

YOU WILL NEED

For one doughnut pincushion:

6×12-inch piece tan, brown, or light brown felt (doughnut pincushion)

5-inch square pink, brown, white, or tan felt (icing appliqué)

Chopstick (optional)

Polyester fiberfill

Embroidery needle

Perle cotton No. 5 or 8: dark pink, cream, white, caramel, yellow

Assorted bugle or seed beads for embellishing (optional)

Finished Pincushion: 4-inch diameter, 1¼ inches tall

Measurements include ¼-inch seam allowances unless otherwise indicated. Sew with right sides together unless otherwise stated. See #092, and the patterns on next page.

CUT THE PIECES

From tan, brown, or light brown felt, cut:

2 of Pattern A (doughnut)

From pink, brown, white, or tan felt, cut:

1 of Patterns B, C, or D (icing)

1. After cutting out doughnut circles A, cut slit and center hole in each as shown on pattern. Be careful not to cut the center hole too big.

2. Layer tan, brown, or light brown felt A pieces with right sides together, aligning edges. Machine-straight-stitch outside curved edges, then inner curved edges, backstitching at beginning and end, to make a tube (Diagram 1).

3. Turn tube right side out and gently push out edges with a chopstick or the eraser end of a pencil.

4. Stuff firmly with fiberfill until tube ends start to come together. Insert one tube end into the other. Using matching thread, slip-stitch overlapped edges together to make a doughnut pincushion (Diagram 2). **Note:** Sew stitches close together, especially in the doughnut center, to create a secure seam.

5. If desired, stitch large cross-stitches or whipstitches around outside curve of doughnut pincushion, using contrasting or matching perle cotton.

6. Position a pink, brown, white, or tan felt B, C, or D icing appliqué on doughnut pincushion (Diagram 3).

7. Using contrasting or matching perle cotton, whipstitch, cross-stitch, or blanket-stitch outside edge of appliqué.

8. Using same color of perle cotton as used in Step 2, whipstitch inside edge of appliqué, pushing appliqué down into curve of doughnut pincushion with your thumb while stitching to complete pincushion. **Note:** Avoid using decorative stitches on the inside edge; this can distort the doughnut.

9. If desired, add "sprinkles" made of perle cotton straight stitches, seed beads sewn on with perle cotton, or bugle beads sewn on with sewing thread. Or, using perle cotton, place vertical straight stitches next to each other to form a diagonal line of "drizzled icing."

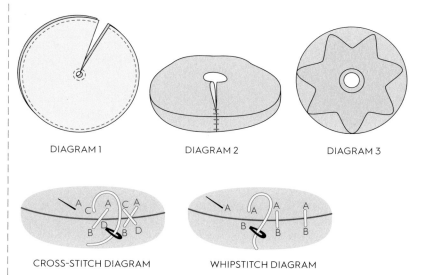

DIAGRAM 1   DIAGRAM 2   DIAGRAM 3

CROSS-STITCH DIAGRAM   WHIPSTITCH DIAGRAM

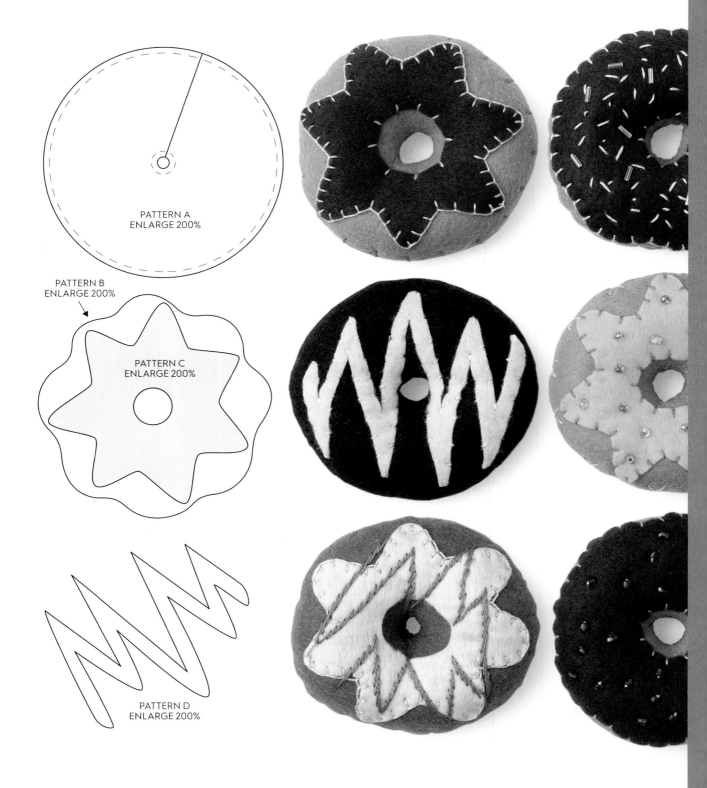

PATTERN A
ENLARGE 200%

PATTERN B
ENLARGE 200%

PATTERN C
ENLARGE 200%

PATTERN D
ENLARGE 200%

035
pin it on the turtle

YOU WILL NEED

Scraps of assorted green solids, dots, and checks (turtle top)

6-inch square green crafts felt (turtle base)

Embroidery floss: black

Polyester fiberfill

4-inch square cardboard

Finished Pincushion: 4×4¾ inches

Measurements include ¼-inch seam allowances unless otherwise indicated. Sew with right sides together unless otherwise indicated.

Make templates of Patterns D and E on Pattern Page B. Transfer dots on patterns to templates, then to fabric pieces. The dots are matching points and are necessary when joining pieces and setting in seams.

CUT THE PIECES

From assorted green solids, dots, and checks, cut:

1 of Pattern D; 6 of Pattern E

From green felt, cut:

1 of Pattern F

From cardboard, cut:

1 of Pattern G

ASSEMBLE PINCUSHION

1. With right sides together, pin together a green solid, dot, or check E piece and the green solid, dot, or check D piece, matching dots. Sew together between dots; do not sew into seam allowances at either end (Diagram 1). Finger-press seam open. Repeat with a second green solid, dot,

or check E piece on adjacent edge of D piece (Diagram 2).

2. Beginning at inside corner, sew E pieces together along short edges. Finger-press seam open.

3. Repeat Steps 1 and 2 to add remaining green solid, dot, or check E pieces to D piece, stitching short edges together after you add each piece (Diagram 3). Press under ¼-inch seam allowance on outer edges to make turtle top.

4. Place turtle top right side down. Layer cardboard G piece and green felt F piece on wrong side of turtle top and turn over. Whipstitch turtle top to felt on all edges, leaving an opening for stuffing (Diagram 4). To whipstitch, bring needle up at A and push it down at B (Whipstitch Diagram). Come up at C and continue around entire shape in same manner.

5. Stuff firmly with fiberfill. Whipstitch opening closed.

6. Use black embroidery floss and small stitches to add eyes and a smile to turtle head and complete the turtle pincushion.

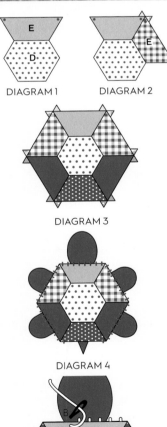

E
D

DIAGRAM 1

E

DIAGRAM 2

DIAGRAM 3

DIAGRAM 4

B
C A

WHIPSTITCH DIAGRAM

036
house your pins

Quickly hand-stitch a tiny village of whimsical felt pincushion houses.

YOU WILL NEED

3-inch square brown crafts felt (window and door appliqués)

6×10-inch rectangle gold crafts felt (house)

4×6-inch rectangle red crafts felt (roof)

Embroidery floss: white, gold, red

Polyester fiberfill

6×10-inch rectangle cardboard

Adhesive tape

Finished Pincushion:
3⅛×1½×3½ inches

CUT THE PIECES

From brown felt, cut:
2—½×¾ inch rectangles (windows)
1 of Pattern A (door), right

From gold felt, cut:
2—3⅜×2¾-inch rectangles (front and back)
1—1¾×3⅜-inch rectangle (bottom)
2—1¾×2¾-inch rectangles (sides)

From red felt, cut:
2 each of Patterns B and C (roof), right

From cardboard, cut:
2—3⅛×2½-inch rectangles (front and back)
1—1½×3⅛-inch rectangle (bottom)
2—1½×2½-inch rectangles (sides)

ASSEMBLE PINCUSHION

1. Referring to Diagram 1, position brown felt ½×¾-inch windows and A door shape on one gold felt 3⅜×2¾-inch rectangle. Referring to photo, opposite, use one strand of white embroidery floss to hand-stitch around window and door edges to make house front.

2. Using two strands of gold embroidery floss, blanket-stitch gold felt 1¾×2¾-inch rectangles to each side edge of house front to make a row (Diagram 2). Blanket-stitch remaining gold felt 3⅜×2¾-inch rectangle to one end of row, then blanket-stitch ends of row together to make a tube-shape house unit.

To blanket-stitch, bring needle up at A (Blanket Stitch Diagram, below), form a reverse L shape with the floss and hold angle of L shape in place with your thumb. Push the needle down at B and come up at C. Continue in same manner.

3. Referring to Diagram 3, use two strands of red embroidery floss to blanket-stitch red felt B pieces to

each short edge of one red felt C piece. Add remaining red felt C piece to remaining short edges of B pieces to make roof unit.

4. Referring to photo, opposite, use two strands of red embroidery floss to blanket-stitch roof unit to house unit.

5. Referring to Diagram 4, use tape to secure two cardboard 3⅛×2½-inch rectangles and two 1½×2½-inch rectangles together, forming a tube-shape cardboard unit.

6. Insert cardboard unit into Step 4 unit. Stuff firmly with fiberfill. Tape cardboard 1½×3⅛-inch piece to bottom of cardboard unit. Blanket-stitch gold felt 1¾×3⅜-inch rectangle to bottom edges of Step 4 unit to complete house pincushion.

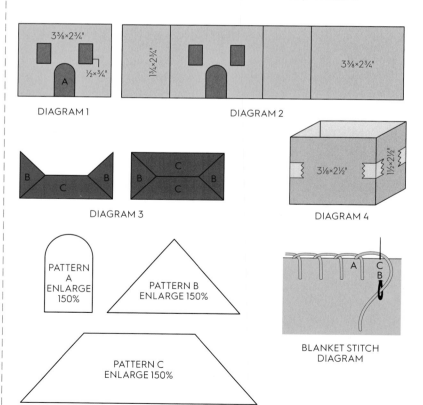

DIAGRAM 1

DIAGRAM 2

3⅛×2¾"

½×¾"

A

1¾×2¾"

3⅜×2¾"

DIAGRAM 3

B   B
C
B   C   B
C

DIAGRAM 4

3⅛×2½"

1½×2½"

PATTERN A ENLARGE 150%

PATTERN B ENLARGE 150%

PATTERN C ENLARGE 150%

A   C
B

BLANKET STITCH DIAGRAM

037
zip up some sweet caddies

Here's a recipe for macaron look-alikes that doesn't require you to be a pastry chef. Sew these caddies from fabric, using plastic circles and polyester fiberfill to get the cookie shape. Add a zipper to resemble the filling; when closed it will hold jewelry or other small valuables.

YOU WILL NEED

6×1-inch rectangle solid pastel (zipper tab, pocket)

2—6×12-inch rectangles solid pastel (outer case, lining)

Heavy-duty template plastic

Heavy paper

Hand-sewing needle and thread

9-inch-long zipper: white

Heavy-duty thread

Finished Caddies: 3-inch diameter

Measurements include ¼-inch seam allowances. Sew with right sides together unless otherwise indicated.

Patterns are on Pattern Page B.

CUT THE PIECES

From solid pastel 1, cut:
2 of Pattern C
1½ inch square

From solid pastel 2, cut:
4 of Pattern A

From template plastic and heavy paper, cut:
2 each of Pattern B

PREPARE ZIPPER UNIT

1. Using needle and thread, secure zipper tape ends ¼-inch below teeth at zipper bottom with overlapping backstitches. Repeat stitching at opposite zipper end ¼ inch from zipper stop.

2. To create the join between the case front and back, fold opposite edges of solid pastel 1, 1½-inch square under ⅜ inch to make a ¾×1½-inch folded unit. Open zipper slightly. Center folded unit on wrong side of zipper over joined zipper ends. Stitch folded edges of unit to zipper tape (A). Close zipper.

3. Turn zipper so zipper pull tab is on the outside. Snip ¼ inch clips every ½ inch around the zipper tape on both sides (B).

ASSEMBLE OUTER CASE

1. Sew gathering stitches close to outer edge of a solid pastel 2 A circle. Place circle right side down on a flat surface. Place a small handful of polyester fiberfill on wrong side of pastel circle. Layer plastic B circle on polyester fiberfill. Pull gathering

thread around plastic circle (enclosing fiberfill) and secure thread ends to make a cover unit (C).

2. Position cover unit on one side of zipper unit. Working from right side, whipstitch cover unit to zipper tape (D). To whipstitch, see Whipstitch Diagram in #035.

3. Using a solid pastel 2 A circle, repeat Step 1 to assemble a second cover unit. Position cover unit atop remaining side of zipper unit. Whipstitch cover unit to zipper tape as before to make outer case.

ASSEMBLE LINING

1. Turn under straight edge of solid pastel 1 C piece ½ inch twice. Topstitch along first fold to make pocket piece. Repeat to make a second pocket piece.

2. Center pocket piece, right side up, atop right side of a solid pastel 2 A circle; baste edges (E).

3. Center a paper B circle on wrong side of solid pastel 2 A circle. Sew gathering stitches close to outer edge of A circle. Place circle right side down on a flat surface. Pull gathering thread around paper circle and secure thread ends to make lining with pocket (F).

4. Repeat Steps 2 and 3 with remaining pocket piece, paper B circle, and solid pastel 2 A circle.

FINISH CASE

Open outer case. Center one lining piece on inside of case. Whipstitch lining to zipper tape (G). Repeat with remaining lining piece on other inside of case to complete case.

A

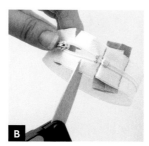

B

C

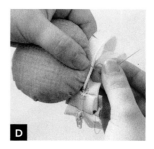

D

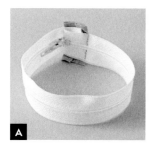

E

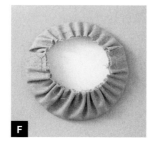

F

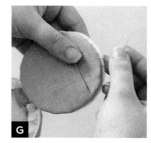

G

038
sprout a mushroom case

Tuck scissors, needles, and a spool of thread into this adorable mushroom-shape needle case.

YOU WILL NEED

5×20-inch rectangle white felted wool (stem pocket, appliqués, needle flaps)

4×12-inch rectangle red felted wool (mushroom cap)

½×3-inch strip aqua felted wool (loop)

Embroidery floss: red and white

Finished Needle Case: 5×6½ inches (excluding loop)

Felted wool is available in many quilt shops. If you want to felt your own wool, machine-wash it in a hot-water wash, cool-rinse cycle with a small amount of detergent; machine-dry on high heat and steam-press.

Patterns are on Pattern Page C. To make paper templates, trace each pattern on paper and cut out. Pin patterns to felted wool and cut around the edges. Because felted wool pieces won't fray, there's no need to add seam allowances or turn under edges.

CUT THE PIECES:

From white wool, cut:
1 each of Patterns A and B
2 of Pattern C
9 of Pattern E

From red wool, cut:
2 of Pattern D

ASSEMBLE NEEDLE CASE

Use two plies of embroidery floss to finish the edges of all felted wool pieces and assemble the pieces in the following steps.

glue it

When appliquéing with wool, use tiny dots of fabric-basting glue to secure small appliqué pieces in place before stitching.

1. Using red floss, blanket-stitch around a red wool D mushroom cap beginning at green dot and ending at white dot, attaching cap to white wool A stem (Diagram 1).

To blanket-stitch, pull needle up at A (Blanket-Stitch Diagram), form a reverse L shape with the floss, and hold the angle of the L shape in place with your thumb. Push needle down at B and come up at C to secure stitch. Continue in same manner.

2. Using white floss, blanket-stitch top edge of white wool B stem beginning at green dot and ending at white dot (Diagram 2).

3. Using white floss, blanket-stitch white wool B stem to white wool A stem beginning at green dot and ending at white dot, joining side and bottom edges of stem pieces and sewing top edge to red cap, to make stem pocket and mushroom back (Diagram 3).

4. Using white floss, blanket-stitch around the outer edges of each white wool C piece.

5. Referring to Appliqué Placement Diagram, position white wool E circles on remaining red wool D mushroom cap. Trim circles even with edges of cap where necessary. Using white floss, blanket-stitch around edges to appliqué E circles.

6. Fold aqua wool ½×3-inch strip in half crosswise. Place mushroom back, pocket side up, on flat surface. Referring to Diagram 4, stack white wool C pieces (needle flaps) together and position on mushroom back. Insert folded aqua wool strip between C pieces with ends extending into center of C pieces about ¼ inch. Position appliquéd D piece on top; pin layers.

7. Using red floss, blanket-stitch the edge of appliquéd D piece only, beginning at green dot and working counterclockwise toward white dot (Diagram 4). At white dot, continue blanket-stitching through all layers to join pieces. End stitching at green dot to complete needle case.

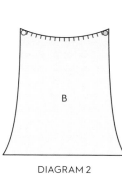

A hidden pocket keeps scissors safe, too!

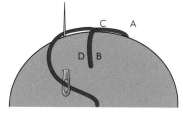

BLANKET-STITCH DIAGRAM

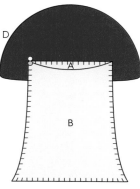

APPLIQUÉ PLACEMENT DIAGRAM

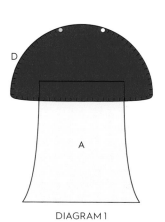

DIAGRAM 1

DIAGRAM 2

DIAGRAM 3

DIAGRAM 4

039
construct a pincushion tower

These quick-to-make pincushions are cute enough to give individually or as a towering set of three.

YOU WILL NEED

Scraps of assorted black-and-white prints

Embroidery floss: black

Cotton or polyester fiberfill

Long, sharp needle (such as a dollmaker's needle)

Yo-Yos

Finished Pincushions: 5½-inch-, 4-inch-, and 2½-inch-diameter

Quantities are for 100% cotton fabrics.

Measurements include ¼-inch seam allowances unless otherwise indicated. Sew with right sides together unless otherwise indicated.

Instructions are given to make one large pincushion. For medium or small size, refer to measurements and patterns in parentheses.

Patterns are on Pattern Page D. To make templates of Patterns A and D

for large pincushion (B and E for medium; C and F for small), see Make Templates and Use Templates in #093.

CUT THE PIECES

From assorted black-and-white prints, cut:

2—7-inch squares (5-inch squares; 3-inch squares)
1 of Pattern D (E; F)

ASSEMBLE PINCUSHION

1. On wrong side of a black-and-white print 7-inch square (5-inch square; 3-inch square), trace around A (B; C) template with a pencil.

2. With right sides together, layer marked and unmarked squares. With a small stitch length (1.5–2 mm), sew on marked line. Overlap stitches slightly where you begin and end.

3. Trim seam allowance a scant ¼ inch beyond stitching line. Clip corners and curves almost to stitching (Diagram 1).

4. Decide which print will be the top of the pincushion; on that side, carefully cut a ¾-inch-long slit in the center (Diagram 1).

5. Turn pincushion right side out. Stuff

tightly with fiberfill (use eraser end of a pencil to poke stuffing into petals). Hand-stitch opening closed.

FINISH PINCUSHION

1. Using six strands of black floss and a long, sharp needle, insert needle into pincushion's top center and bring it out at bottom center (Diagram 2). Bring floss up around one of the inside curves between petals, then push needle from top center down to bottom center as before. Continue stitching and wrapping floss between all petals, pulling tightly to indent pincushion. Knot securely.

2. Turn under ¼ inch around black-and-white print D (E; F) circle. Using a long running stitch, hand-stitch close to folded edge; draw up stitches tightly and tie thread ends in a knot to make a yo-yo (Diagram 3). (To speed process, use large, small, and extra-small yo-yo-making tools available at quilt shops and crafts supply stores.)

3. Hand-stitch yo-yo to top center of pincushion with matching thread to complete pincushion.

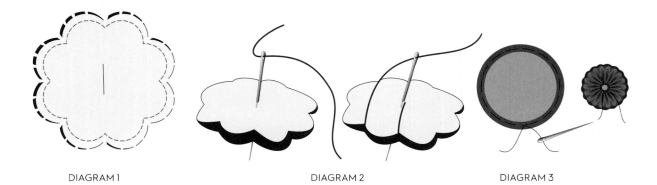

DIAGRAM 1   DIAGRAM 2   DIAGRAM 3

add color

Polka dots and stripes in hot, bright colors give these pincushions a fun, contemporary look. Switch fabric colors and turn them into spring blooms. Or use holiday prints to make poinsettia pincushions. Create simple ornaments using print fabrics that evoke Victorian designs and the medium and small pincushion templates. Attach a thin gold cord for a hanger.

040
take a to-go bag

Use a single appliqué shape to adorn a take-along sewing kit.

YOU WILL NEED

Scraps of green, brown, and aqua prints (appliqués)

9×21-inch piece (fat eighth) cream print (bag body, lining)

Freezer paper

Fabric glue stick

9-inch-long zipper: cream

Finished Bag: 7½×4 inches

Measurements include ¼-inch seam allowances unless otherwise indicated. Sew with right sides together unless otherwise indicated.

The pattern is on Pattern Page K.

CUT THE PIECES

From each green, brown, and aqua print scrap, cut:

1 of Circle Pattern

From cream print, cut:

4—4½×8-inch rectangles for bag body and lining.

1. Lay freezer paper, shiny side down, over Circle Pattern. Trace the pattern three times with a pencil. Cut out freezer-paper shapes on drawn lines.

2. Place a small amount of fabric glue on dull side of freezer-paper shapes; position each shape on wrong side of a print scrap. Cut out each shape, adding a ³⁄₁₆-inch seam allowance to circle edge. Clip seam allowances of curves as necessary, stopping a thread or two away from freezer paper.

3. Using tip of a hot dry iron, press seam allowance of each circle over edge onto shiny side of freezer paper; let cool.

APPLIQUÉ CIRCLES

1. Remove freezer paper from prepared circle appliqués.

2. Referring to Appliqué Placement Diagram, arrange circle appliqués on a cream print 4½×8-inch rectangle; glue-baste in place.

3. Using small slip stitches, hand-appliqué circles in place to make bag body front.

ASSEMBLE BAG

1. Place a cream print 4½×8-inch lining rectangle, right side up, on a flat surface. Center and align cream zipper faceup along one long edge of rectangle. Place bag body front facedown on top of zipper; pin together through all three layers.

2. Using a zipper foot and a ¼-inch seam allowance, stitch layers together (Diagram 1).

3. Finger-press bag body front and lining away from zipper. Topstitch a scant ¼ inch from fold to make front unit (Diagram 2).

4. Using remaining cream print 4½×8-inch rectangles, repeat Steps 1 through 3 to stitch remaining zipper edge and make back unit.

5. Move zipper tab to center of zipper.

6. Open up front unit and back unit. With right sides together, layer front and back units so bag body front and back are together and lining front and back are together; pin. Join units around all edges, leaving a 3-inch opening in lining for turning (Diagram 3).

7. Turn units right side out through opening in lining and finger-press seams. Slip-stitch lining opening closed. Insert lining into bag body to complete bag.

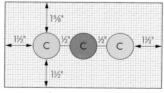

APPLIQUÉ PLACEMENT DIAGRAM

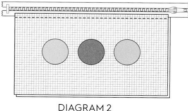

DIAGRAM 2

DIAGRAM 1

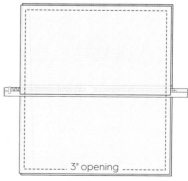

DIAGRAM 3

—Make in Minutes—

Keep your sewing space neat and clean by making a set of these mini thread catcher bags.
Those clipped threads won't stand a chance!

041
scale down your storage

YOU WILL NEED

9×21-inch piece (fat eighth) aqua house print (bag body)

7-inch square cream-and-aqua circle print (bag body)

2×13-inch strip cream-and-aqua leaf print (flange)

9×21-inch piece (fat eighth) aqua stripe (bag lining)

6½×17½-inch rectangle fusible fleece

Finished Bag: 7¼×3×3 inches

Yardages and cutting instructions are based on 42 inches of usable fabric width.

Measurements include ¼-inch seam allowances unless otherwise indicated. Sew with right sides together unless otherwise indicated.

CUT THE PIECES

From aqua house print, cut:
2—6½-inch squares

From cream-and-aqua circle print, cut:
1—6½×5½-inch-rectangle

From cream-and-aqua leaf print, cut:
1—1¼×12½-inch strip

From aqua stripe, cut:
1—6½×17½-inch rectangle

ASSEMBLE BAG

1. Sew together two aqua house print 6½-inch squares and the cream-and-aqua circle print 6½×5½-inch rectangle to make a pieced rectangle (Diagram 1). If using a directional fabric, make sure the pieces face in opposite directions so when the pieced rectangle is folded, the fabrics are oriented correctly. Press seams open. The pieced rectangle should be 6½×17½ inches including seam allowances.

2. Following manufacturer's instructions, fuse 6½×17½-inch fleece rectangle to Step 1 pieced rectangle.

3. Quilt if desired.

4. With right side inside, fold fused pieced rectangle in half crosswise and press fold to make a placement line; the folded rectangle should measure 6½×8¾ inches. Sew together pairs of long edges to make bag body (Diagram 2). Clip into seam allowance at placement line in order to press seams open.

5. To shape a flat bottom for bag body, at one corner match side seam with pressed placement line, creating a flattened triangle (Diagram 3). Measuring 1½ inches

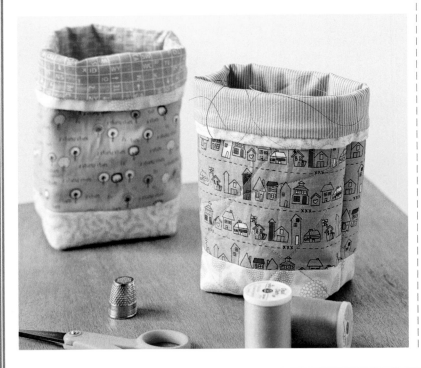

from point of triangle, draw a 3-inch-long line across triangle; sew on drawn line. Trim excess fabric ¼ inch from stitching line. Repeat with remaining bottom corner. Turn bag body right side out; press.

6. With wrong side inside, press cream-and-aqua leaf print 1¼×12½-inch strip in half lengthwise; unfold. Join short ends to make a tube (Diagram 4). Press seam open. Turn tube right side out and fold back in half using pressed line as a guide.

7. Matching raw edges, place tube around top edge of bag body. Pin in place. Baste using ⅛-inch seam allowance (Diagram 5).

8. With right side inside, fold aqua stripe 6½×17½-inch rectangle in half crosswise; the folded rectangle should measure 6½×8¾ inches. Sew together pairs of long edges, leaving a 3-inch opening in one seam for turning, to make bag lining.

9. Repeat Step 5 to shape a flat bottom for bag lining. Do not turn lining right side out.

10. Insert bag body into bag lining with right sides together. Align raw edges and seams. Sew together top edges of bag body and lining. Turn right side out through opening in lining. Pull lining out of bag body; hand-stitch opening closed. Insert lining back into bag body and fold down top edge to complete.

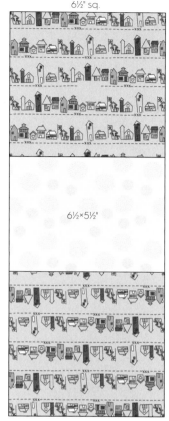

6½" sq.

6½×5½"

DIAGRAM 1

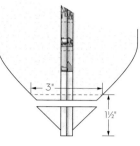

3"

1½"

DIAGRAM 3

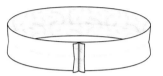

DIAGRAM 4

DIAGRAM 5

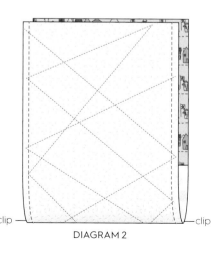

clip   clip

DIAGRAM 2

Purses, Bags & Accessories

Keep your essentials contained and easy to find with custom carry-alls to store everything you need at home and on the go.

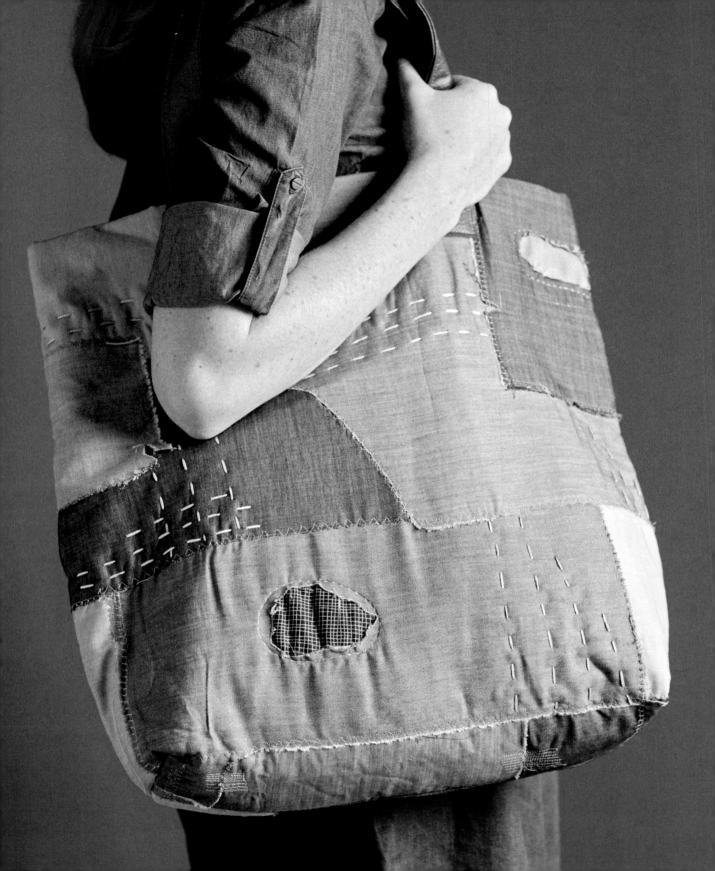

042
design a custom carry-all

This roomy denim tote is the perfect accessory for shopping or carrying everyday must-haves. Create the patchwork look by ripping and fraying pieces of denim and coordinating prints, arranging the pieces like a collage, then sewing the pieces in place with various decorative stitches.

YOU WILL NEED

2 yards total of four assorted shades lightweight blue denim

Scraps of blue and gray prints

2—20-inch squares quilt batting

Sewing thread: cream, light brown, brown

Seam ripper or small scissors

Water-soluble marking pen

No. 5 perle cotton: white, ecru, tan

Size 3, long-eye embroidery needle

2—6×25-inch tan faux-leather strips

Wonder Clips

Jeans needle

2—20×19-inch rectangles lining fabric

Yardages and cutting instructions are based on 42 inches of usable fabric width.

Measurements include ¼-inch seam allowances unless otherwise indicated. Sew with the right sides together unless otherwise indicated.

Finished Tote: 15×17×5 inches

1. Working with one piece of denim at a time, make a small cut parallel to the selvage edge of fabric. Tear at cut to remove selvage. Repeat with remaining fabrics. In a similar manner, clip and tear assorted denims into squares and rectangles in assorted sizes (ours range from 4×6 to 8×16 inches). You will need enough torn pieces to cover each 20-inch square batting with edges of denim overlapping. Use your fingertips or an emery board to rough up and unravel torn edges.

2. Lay out one piece of quilt batting on a flat surface. Arrange and overlap assorted torn denim pieces in collage fashion until batting is covered and desired arrangement is achieved (Diagram 1). Tear pieces from corners of some denim as desired. Pin edges of denim pieces to batting.

To make a worn or distressed spot, remove desired piece from layout. Tear a printed fabric scrap slightly smaller than denim piece. Place print fabric scrap under denim with right sides up for both fabrics. Using small running stitches, sew an oval or rectangle shape through both layers (Diagram 2). Cut a small hole within stitched shape on denim using a seam ripper or small scissors to expose the print fabric. Repin modified denim piece on batting.

3. Sew denim to batting, about ¼ inch from edges, using assorted decorative machine stitches such as darning stitch, tricot stitch, running stitch, triple stitch, and triple zigzag stitch. Change stitches and thread color as desired. Using a long straight stitch, sew through all layers ¼ inch from outer edges of piece. Trim, if necessary, to 20-inch square.

4. Using water-soluble marking pen, mark lines as desired on the bag piece as guides for large stitches. Using two strands of perle cotton, make ⅜-inch-long running stitches along marked lines. Change colors of perle cotton as desired.

5. Repeat Steps 2 and 3 to make and stitch a second 20-inch square piece.

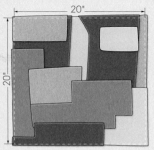

DIAGRAM 1

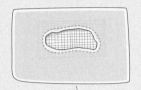

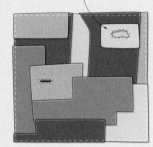

DIAGRAM 2

DIAGRAM 3

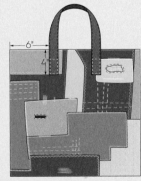

DIAGRAM 4

6. With wrong side inside, fold 6×25-inch faux-leather strip in half lengthwise; finger-press. Open strip and fold long edges to meet at creased center (Diagram 3, previous page). Fold again along center crease to make a 1½×25-inch strip; finger-press. Hold folded edges together with Wonder Clips. (Pins will leave permanent holes in the faux leather.)

7. Replace standard machine needle with jeans needle. Beginning at one end of strip, edgestitch ¼ inch from both long edges of strip to make a strap (Diagram 3, previous page). Remove clips just before the needle reaches them.

8. Repeat Steps 6 and 7 to make a second strap.

9. Position ends of one strap on a bag piece 6 inches from side edges and 4 inches from top edge (Diagram 4, previous page). Using water-soluble marking pen, trace around strap end positions. Working with one end of strap at a time, align strap end at marked position. Hold in place with one hand as you sew a 2×2½-inch rectangle through all layers. Repeat with remaining strap end.

10. Repeat Step 9 with other bag piece and strap. Replace jeans needle with a standard machine needle.

11. Mark a 3-inch square at bottom corners of each bag piece; cut out squares (Diagram 5).

12. With right sides together, sew bag front to bag back along side and bottom edges (Diagram 6).

13. Fold pieces so bottom seam aligns with corresponding side seam (Diagram 7). Stitch across end to make bag base. Repeat with other side of bag to make outer bag. Do not turn right side out.

14. Using 20×19-inch lining pieces, repeat Steps 11 through 13, leaving a 5-inch opening along one side edge. Turn lining right side out.

15. Place lining inside outer bag with right sides together and side seams matching; pin (Diagram 8). Stitch along top edges. Turn right side out through opening in lining; then pull lining out of outer bag. Hand-stitch opening closed. Push lining inside outer bag.

Note: 1 inch of outer bag folds to inside bag at top edge. Press top edge, avoiding touching faux leather with iron.

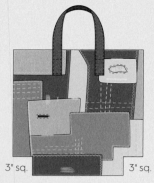

3" sq.   3" sq.

DIAGRAM 5

DIAGRAM 6

DIAGRAM 7

lining

bag

DIAGRAM 8

043
cook in style

Embellish an apron and add function with help from a pocket salvaged from a pair of jeans. The apron whips up quickly using a simple folding and cutting technique. The jean pocket itself is useful for stashing a small item, and the large contrasting pocket has plenty of room for holding more items as you cook.

YOU WILL NEED

1 yard lightweight solid blue denim (apron)

1 yard lightweight dark print blue denim (pocket, strap)

Old jeans: one back pocket

Jeans needle

Yardages and cutting instructions are based on 42 inches of usable fabric width.

Measurements include ¼-inch seam allowances unless otherwise indicated. Sew with right sides together unless otherwise indicated.

Finished Apron: 23×28 inches

CUT THE PIECES

From solid blue denim, cut:

1—25×32-inch rectangle

From dark print blue denim, cut:

1—18-inch square

4—2×42-inch strips

1. Trace armhole pattern from Pattern Page F onto paper; enlarge and cut out. Fold 25×32-inch solid blue denim rectangle in half vertically. Place armhole pattern on folded fabric as shown in Diagram 1; cut out.

2. Fold 18-inch dark print blue denim square in half with right sides together to make a 9×18-inch rectangle. Sew ¼-inch seam on raw edges, leaving a 3-inch opening in center of one short edge for turning (Diagram 2). Turn right side out and press. Stitch opening closed. Edgestitch along folded edge of pocket piece. Topstitch a scant ¼ inch from first row of stitching.

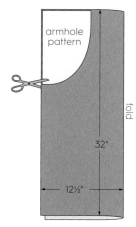

DIAGRAM 1

DIAGRAM 2

DIAGRAM 3

3. Using sharp scissors, cut a pocket from old jeans, cutting very close to pocket at side and bottom edges and leaving 1 inch of jeans fabric at top edge (Diagram 3).

4. Turn 1 inch of jeans fabric to back side of jeans pocket; press.

5. Fold Step 2 pocket piece in half; finger-crease. Position jeans pocket in center of left half of pocket piece. Pin jeans pocket to pocket piece through edges of turned-under fabric (Diagram 4).

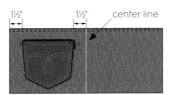

DIAGRAM 4

6. Replace standard machine needle with jeans needle. Flip up jeans pocket. Sew jeans pocket to pocket piece from Step 2 along fold of jeans pocket flap (Diagram 5).

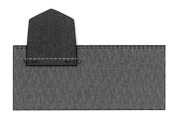

DIAGRAM 5

7. Flip jeans pocket down; pin in place. Topstitch jeans pocket side

and bottom edges through all layers following jeans pocket stitching lines to complete pocket (Diagram 6).

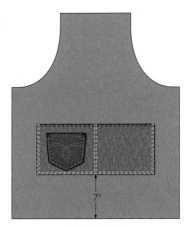

DIAGRAM 6

8. Pin pocket in place 7 inches from bottom edge of apron front. Edgestitch bottom and side edges of pocket; topstitch a scant ¼ inch from outer pocket edges (Diagram 7). Add two vertical rows of stitching at pocket center. Replace jeans needle with standard machine needle.

DIAGRAM 7

9. Turn under apron's side edges ½ inch twice; press. Edgestitch and topstitch a scant ½ inch from folded edges. Repeat with top and bottom edges, turning edges under 1 inch twice before stitching

10. Join four 2×42-inch strips to make one long strap. Trim to 145 inches.

11. With wrong side inside, fold strip in half lengthwise; press. Open strip and fold long edges to meet at creased center (Diagram 8). Fold

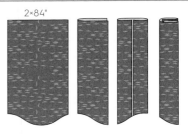

DIAGRAM 8

again along center crease to make a ½×145-inch strap; press.

12. Fold strap in half; lightly press to mark center. Measure and mark 12 inches to left side of center crease. Align marked position on strip with top left-hand edge of apron body (Diagram 9). Sandwich raw edge of apron armhole in strip fold; pin strip in place along curved edge. Measuring 12 inches to right side of center crease, align strip with top right-hand edge of apron body; pin strip along remaining armhole.

DIAGRAM 9

13. Edgestitch a scant ⅛ inch from both edges of strip to secure strap. Tie a knot at each end to complete.

—Make in Minutes—

Customize an infinity scarf by choosing the perfect print for each person on your list, then give it a custom finish with a fun pom-pom fringe.

044
embellish a scarf

YOU WILL NEED

2¼ yards multicolor print

2⅛ yards pom-pom trim

Finished Scarf: approximately 73 inches around

Sew with ¼-inch seam allowances and right sides together. Cut multicolor print rectangle lengthwise (parallel to the selvage).

CUT THE PIECES

From multicolor print, cut:

1—14×73½-inch strip

1. Fold the strip in half lengthwise with right sides together. With the pom-pom trim edge aligned along the fabric raw edge, pin and sew the pom-pom fringe to the long edges of the strip to make a tube. Turn the tube right side out.

2. Lay the tube flat on work surface. Pick up one end of the tube and flip it over, creating a twist (Diagram 1).

3. Fold the tube in half by turning one end wrong side out and pulling it over the opposite end until the short ends are aligned (Diagram 2).

4. Sew around the short ends, leaving 4 inches open (Diagram 3).

5. Turn the scarf right side out through the opening. Hand-sew the opening closed.

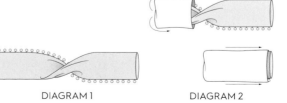

DIAGRAM 1   DIAGRAM 2   DIAGRAM 3

make it yours

Pick fabric that fits the season, your mood, or that coordinates with other accessories. Or try a map-inspired print or theme fabric to remind you of a favorite place.

045
travel light

Here's the perfect on-the-go bag with pockets for plenty of storage.

MATERIALS

¼ yard blue large floral (bag front, bag back, inner pocket lining)

½ yard blue dot (outer pocket, inner pocket, strap, triangle flap)

¼ yard light blue batik (bag lining, outer pocket lining)

¼ yard blue small floral (binding)

Double-sided fusible fleece

Sew-in magnetic snap set

¾-inch-diameter button: dark blue

Finished Bag: 7¼×9 inches (excluding strap)

Yardages and cutting instructions are based on 42 inches of usable fabric width.

Measurements include ¼-inch seam allowances unless otherwise indicated. Sew with right sides together unless otherwise indicated.

CUT THE PIECES

From blue large floral, cut:
2—7¼×9-inch rectangles
1—7×7¼-inch rectangle

From blue dot, cut:
2—2×42-inch strips
2—6½×7¼-inch rectangles
1—3¾×7-inch rectangle

From light blue batik, cut:
2—7¼×9-inch rectangles
1—7×7¼-inch rectangle

From blue small floral, cut:
1—2×42-inch binding strip
2—2×7¼-inch binding strips

From double-sided fusible fleece, cut:
2—½×42-inch strips
2—7¼×9-inch rectangles
2—6½×7¼-inch rectangles

BAG FRONT AND BACK UNITS

1. Layer a blue large floral 7¼×9-inch rectangle, right side up; a fusible fleece 7¼×9-inch rectangle; and a light blue batik 7¼×9-inch rectangle, right side down (Diagram 1). Following manufacturer's instructions, fuse layers together to make a fused rectangle. Repeat with remaining fabric and fleece 7¼×9-inch rectangles to make a second fused rectangle.

2. Referring to Diagram 2, machine-quilt two vertical lines 2¼ inches from each long edge of a fused rectangle. Baste ⅛ inch from outside edges to make bag front unit. Repeat with remaining fused rectangle to make bag back unit.

OUTER AND INNER POCKET UNITS

1. Layer a fusible fleece 6½×7¼-inch rectangle atop wrong side of a blue dot 6½×7¼-inch rectangle; fuse together. With right sides together, lay fused blue dot rectangle atop light blue batik 7×7¼-inch rectangle, aligning one long edge. The light blue batik rectangle will be ½ inch longer than the fused rectangle. Sew together along aligned edge (Diagram 3). Turn right side out, matching unsewn bottom edges, and press top fold; ¼ inch of pocket lining will show along top edge of pocket front. Topstitch through all layers in the seam line to make an outer pocket unit **(Diagram 4, next page).**

2. Using remaining fusible fleece 6½×7¼-inch rectangle, blue dot 6½×7¼-inch rectangle, and blue large floral 7×7¼-inch rectangle, repeat Step 1 to make inner pocket unit.

STRAP

1. Join two blue dot 2×42-inch strips along short edges to make a

7¼×9"

DIAGRAM 1

2¼"   2¼"

DIAGRAM 2

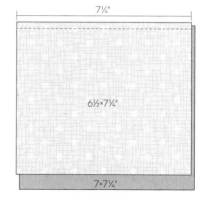

7¼"

6½×7¼"

7×7¼"

DIAGRAM 3

➲ 2×83½-inch pieced strip; press seam open. Fold pieced strip in half lengthwise, wrong side inside. Press to crease center; unfold. Fold long edges of pieced strip to meet in center (Diagram 5). Fold again at center, matching folded edges; press.

2. Open Step 1 strip and place fusible fleece ½×42-inch strips close to center fold, abutting ends of fusible fleece strips in center of pieced strip. Refold pieced strip to cover fusible fleece and topstitch ⅛ inch away from both long edges to make strap.

FINISH BAG

1. Lay bag front unit right side up on a flat surface. Place one end of strap on bag front ¾ inch from left side and 4 inches from bottom (Diagram 6). Topstitch ⅛ inch away from edges of strap, pivoting ½ inch from top edge of bag front unit.

2. Aligning side and bottom raw edges, place outer pocket unit atop Step 1 unit. Baste together ⅛ inch away from side and bottom edges (Diagram 7).

3. Lay bag back unit right side up on a flat surface. Match remaining end of strap to bottom edge of bag back unit ¾ inch from left side. Topstitch strap in place as before, pivoting ½ inch from top edge of bag back unit (Diagram 8).

4. Referring to Diagram 9, opposite, layer inner pocket unit atop lining side of bag back unit; baste together ⅛-inch away from side and bottom edges.

5. Press one long edge of blue dot 3¾×7-inch rectangle ¼ inch toward wrong side (Diagram 10, opposite). Fold short ends diagonally to center to make a folded triangle. Topstitch along folds to make triangle flap.

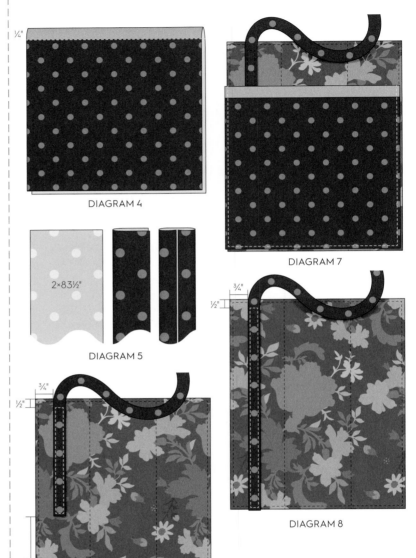

DIAGRAM 4

2×83½"

DIAGRAM 5

DIAGRAM 6

DIAGRAM 7

DIAGRAM 8

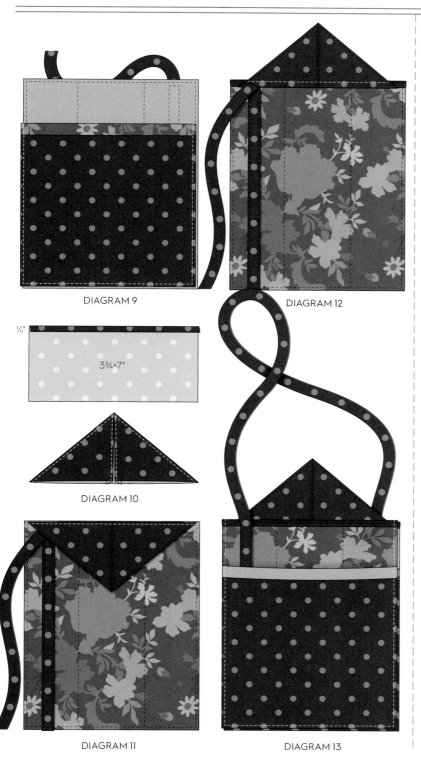

DIAGRAM 9

¼"

3¾×7"

DIAGRAM 10

DIAGRAM 11

DIAGRAM 12

DIAGRAM 13

6. With right sides together, center triangle flap atop bag back unit along top edge. Baste ⅛ inch away from top edge (Diagram 11).

7. Bind top edge of bag front unit using one blue small floral 2×7¼-inch strip. (For details, see #094.) Using remaining blue small floral 2×7¼-inch strip, repeat to bind top edge of bag back unit.

8. Referring to Diagram 12, fold up triangle flap and topstitch to binding on bag back unit.

9. Layer bag front unit and bag back unit with wrong sides together (Diagram 13). (The outer pocket unit will be on the outside, the inner pocket unit will be on the inside, and the strap will be on opposite sides.) Baste together ⅛ inch away from bottom and side edges.

10. Bind side and bottom edges with blue small floral 2×42-inch strip. (For details, see #094.)

11. Following manufacturer's instructions, hand-sew the female end of the magnetic snap to wrong side of triangle flap. Matching position for the male end of the snap, hand-sew it to bag front, making sure snaps fit together when flap is folded.

12. Hand-sew the dark blue button to front side of triangle flap to complete bag.

046
finish with a bow

An oversize fabric bow lends charm to an all-purpose bag that's just right for stashing your essentials. Don't let adding the zipper closure intimidate you—double-stick sewing tape makes it easy.

YOU WILL NEED

3—18×22-inch pieces (fat quarters) in cream print (bag), light blue (lining), navy (bow)

10-inch-long zipper

Lightweight fusible web (such as Heat 'n' Bond Lite)

Double-stick sewing tape (such as Wash Away Wonder Tape)

Finished Bag: 8½×15½ inches

Yardages and cutting instructions are based on 42 inches of usable fabric width.

Measurements include ¼-inch seam allowances unless otherwise indicated. Sew with right sides together unless otherwise indicated.

CUT THE PIECES

From cream print, cut:
2—9×16-inch rectangles (exterior)

From light blue, cut:
2—9×16-inch rectangles (lining)

From navy, cut:
1—16×18-inch rectangle (bow)
1—4×5-inch rectangle (bow loop)

From lightweight fusible web, cut:
2—9×16-inch rectangles

1. Following manufacturer's instructions, press each fusible-web rectangle onto wrong side of each cream print 9×16-inch rectangle; let cool. Peel off paper backings and press fusible-web side of each exterior rectangle onto wrong side of each bag light blue 9×16-inch lining

rectangle to make a bag front and a bag back (Diagram 1); let cool.

2. With right sides together, fold navy 16×18-inch rectangle in half to measure 8×18 inches. Sew along the 18-inch-long side to make a tube (Diagram 2). Turn tube right side out, center the seam on back, and press.

3. With right sides together, fold navy blue 4×5-inch rectangle in half to measure 2½×4 inches. Sew along the 4-inch-long side to make a tube. Turn tube right side out, center the seam on the back, and press. With the seam on the outside, fold tube in half and match short raw edges. Sew the ends together to make a ring (Diagram 3). Turn ring right side out.

4. Carefully insert the tube into the ring. Adjust pieces so the seam for the tube is facing the front and the seam for the ring is facing back.

5. Fold bag front in half crosswise and then lengthwise; finger-press the intersecting fold to find the center; unfold with exterior side faceup. With the wrong side of the bow facedown, center the bow over the center mark and pin the bow ends to the bag sides. Sew bow ends to sides using a scant ¼-inch seam allowance (Diagram 4, next page).

6. Place bag front on a flat surface with bow side facing up. Cut a 16-inch-long piece of double-stick sewing tape. Following the package instructions, press double-stick sewing tape to a 16-inch-long edge of the bag front. Gently peel off tape's paper backing to expose sticky side of tape. **Note:** Wash Away Wonder Tape is available in fabric stores in the notions department.

7. Match right side of zipper to sticky side of tape, pressing with your finger

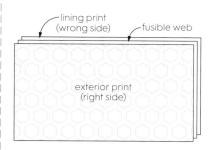

DIAGRAM 1

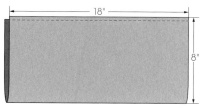

DIAGRAM 2

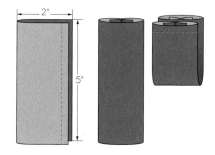

DIAGRAM 3

to secure zipper. Tape will hold the zipper firmly in place without pins. If your machine has a zipper foot, attach it to your sewing machine. If you don't have a zipper foot, you can still sew on a zipper, making the stitching line as near to the zipper teeth as possible. Sew along edge of bag front near zipper teeth (Diagram 5). When you get to the zipper pull, do not swerve to go around it. Instead, stop with the needle down in the fabric, lift presser foot, and slide zipper pull up and out of the way. Lower presser foot and continue sewing.

8. Fold zipper faceup (Diagram 6). Finger-press bag front away from zipper. Repeat Steps 7 and 8 with the bag back, sewing down opposite side of zipper teeth in the same manner. Finger-press as before.

9. Topstitch ⅛ inch from folds on each side of zipper (Diagram 7). **Note:** The sewing tape is temporary and will not gum up your needle.

10. Remove the zipper foot from the sewing machine and replace it with a regular sewing foot. With right sides inside and zipper almost all the way open, fold bag body in half, matching 9-inch-long edges; pin. Sew the sides and bottom (Diagram 8).

11. To shape bottom of bag, at one corner match bottom seam line to side seam line, creating a flattened triangle (Diagram 9). Measuring 2 inches from point of triangle, draw a 2-inch-long line across triangle. Sew on drawn line. Trim excess fabric, leaving ½-inch seam allowance. Repeat with remaining bottom corner of bag.

12. Turn bag right side out through open zipper. Arrange bow pleats as desired.

DIAGRAM 4

DIAGRAM 5

DIAGRAM 6

DIAGRAM 7

DIAGRAM 8

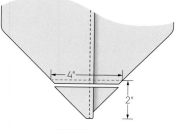

DIAGRAM 9

—Make in Minutes—

Embroider a happy daisy and insert it into a necklace
pendant to usher in the spirit of spring, no matter what time of year it is.

047
grow a flower pendant

YOU WILL NEED

Rectangular necklace pendant (the pendant shown has a ¾×1¾-inch opening)

Ruler

Sewing needle and thread

Gray felt

Chalk pencil

Embroidery floss: green, yellow, gold

Tapestry needle

Crafts glue and small paintbrush

Jump ring

Jewelry tools

Necklace chain

Necklace clasp

1. Measure the opening of the necklace pendant. Using needle and thread, stitch a long running stitch onto the felt to the same dimensions.

Note: By stitching the design area onto the felt before trimming, you will have more felt to hold on to while stitching. These stitches will be used as a guide for centering your embroidery and will be removed later on.

2. Referring to the pattern, right, as a guide, lightly mark the flower stem and flower onto the felt with a chalk pencil, positioning it as desired inside the running-stitch design area. Take care to mark in areas that will be concealed by your stitching.

3. Use three strands of embroidery floss for all stitches. Refer to the pattern to stitch the design. For stitch diagrams and instructions, see #092. Chain-stitch the flower stem. Add lazy daisy stitches at the top of the stem to complete an eight-petal flower, leaving a small area unstitched for the flower center. Add three or four French knots in the flower center. Satin-stitch the leaves.

4. When all embroidery is complete, use scissors to trim the design to the pendant dimensions, cutting through the running-stitch lines. Remove any running stitches that remain.

5. Use a small paintbrush to coat the inside of the necklace pendant with a thin layer of glue. Lightly press the finished embroidery inside the pendant.

6. Attach a jump ring to the pendant. Cut the necklace chain into two pieces that equal the desired length. Attach one end of each chain to the jump ring, then attach the clasp to the other chain ends.

- - - Chain Stitch

— Satin Stitch

● French Knot

⟋ Lazy Daisy Stitch

FULL-SIZE EMBROIDERY PATTERN

048
make a mini bag

Whether for storing notions or essentials for quick trips out of the house, these small bags are perfect.

YOU WILL NEED

½ yard Print A (bag)

¾ yard Print B (lining)

18×44-inch thin quilt batting or crafts fleece

Finished Bag: 13×18 inches

Yardages and cutting instructions are based on 42 inches of usable fabric width.

Measurements include ¼-inch seam allowances unless otherwise indicated. Sew with right sides together unless otherwise indicated.

The pattern is on Pattern Page F. To make a template of pattern, trace it onto a large sheet of paper; enlarge and cut out. Transfer clips and dots onto pattern, then to fabric pieces.

CUT THE PIECES

From Print A, cut:

1 each of Bag Pattern and Bag Pattern reversed

From Print B, cut:

1 each of Bag Pattern and Bag Pattern reversed

2—6½×15-inch rectangles

From batting, cut:

2 of Bag Pattern

1. Layer a batting bag piece on wrong side of each Print A bag piece. Machine-baste a scant ¼ inch from edges to make bag front and back (Diagram 1).

2. Fold a Print B 6½×15-inch rectangle in half lengthwise to make a 3¼×15-inch rectangle. Sew together along three open edges, leaving a

3-inch opening for turning in bottom edge (Diagram 2). Turn right side out through opening. Press, turning under raw edges of opening, to make a pocket. Repeat to make a second pocket.

3. Position a pocket on the right side of each Print B bag piece at the widest part; pin in place. Referring to Diagram 3, topstitch bottom edge of each pocket, then stitch two lines 5 inches apart to divide each pocket into compartments. Trim pocket side edges along curve of bag piece; baste ¼ inch from edges to make lining front and back.

4. With right sides together, sew together bag front and back from clip mark to clip mark along side and bottom edges (Diagram 4). Clip into seam allowance where marked. Turn bag right side out; press flat.

5. Repeat Step 5 to sew together lining front and back, leaving an opening for turning between the dots in the bottom seam (Diagram 5). Do not turn right side out.

6. Insert bag body into lining (right sides together). Sew together bag body and lining along inside and outside edges, beginning and ending 2 inches from top edges (Diagram 6). Pull bag and lining through opening in lining bottom. Hand-stitch opening closed. Push bag into lining (bag wrong sides out).

7. On the lining, carefully press under ¼ inch on the handle upper edges. Keeping the lining out of the way, pin together the long handle ends of the bag body; stitch with ½-inch seam allowance (Diagram 7). Repeat to join the bag body short handle ends.

8. Turn in remaining raw edges of handles on bag body and lining handle (the lining handle ends should overlap each other); pin in place. Turn right side out. Topstitch around all edges to secure the handle ends and complete the bag (Diagram 8).

Loop the short handle over the longer one for wrist-carrying ease.

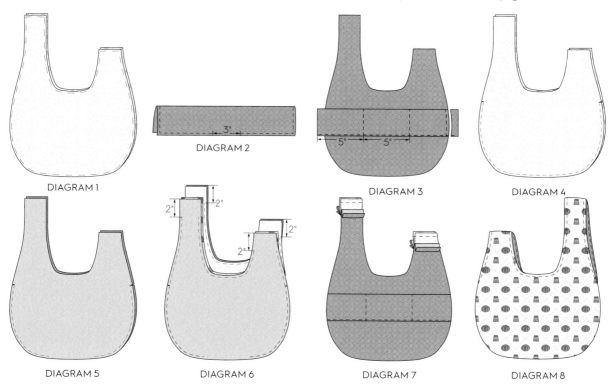

DIAGRAM 1

DIAGRAM 2

DIAGRAM 3

DIAGRAM 4

DIAGRAM 5

DIAGRAM 6

DIAGRAM 7

DIAGRAM 8

049
craft a pretty clutch

A sparkly antique pin at the closure accentuates the feminine shape of a classic handheld purse.

YOU WILL NEED

½ yard green floral (body, tab)

½ yard coordinating print (lining)

½ yard canvas (interlining)

½ yard of 13-inch-wide ultra heavyweight interfacing

1¼ inches of ¾-inch-wide sew-on Velcro

Fabric marker

Pressing ham (optional; available at fabric or sewing stores)

Vintage pin

Finished Clutch: 11¾×7½ inches

Quantities are for 44/45-inch-wide, 100% cotton fabrics.

Measurements include ½-inch seam allowances. Sew with right sides together unless otherwise stated.

Patterns are on Pattern Page G. To make templates of the patterns, see #93. **Note:** When cutting the clutch body and tab pieces (A, B, and D), you may wish to align patterns carefully to match fabric motifs.

CUT THE PIECES

From green floral, cut:
1 each of Patterns A, B, and D

From coordinating print, cut:
1 each of Patterns A, B, and D

From canvas, cut:
1 each of Patterns A, B, and D

From ultra heavyweight interfacing, cut:
2 of Pattern C

ASSEMBLE CLUTCH BODY

1. Referring to Diagram 1, center an interfacing C piece atop wrong side of canvas A piece, leaving ½ inch of canvas exposed around outer edges; pin. **Note:** Interfacing pieces are cut smaller than canvas pieces to reduce bulk in seam allowances and to make it easier to shape sides of clutch.

2. Sew ¼ inch inside edges of interfacing to make a front interfacing unit.

3. Repeat Steps 1 and 2 to sew remaining interfacing C piece atop wrong side of canvas B piece to make a back interfacing unit.

4. Align front interfacing unit, canvas side down, atop wrong side of green floral A piece (Diagram 2); pin. Machine-baste ¼ inch from outer edges to make clutch front.

5. Repeat Step 4 to sew back interfacing unit on wrong side of green floral B piece to make clutch back.

ASSEMBLE AND ADD TAB

The tab on this clutch serves as both a handle on clutch back side (see photo, next spread) and as a closure.

1. Layer canvas D piece on wrong side of green floral D piece; baste ¼ inch from outer edge (Diagram 3).

2. With right sides together, layer Step 1 unit and coordinating print (lining) D piece. Backstitching at beginning and end, sew together long edges, using a ½-inch seam to make tab; leave short edges open for turning (Diagram 3).

3. Trim seam allowances to ⅛ inch. Turn tab right side out by pulling narrow end through wide end; press.

4. Tuck ½ inch of wide end inside tab; press. Tuck ⅜ inch of narrow end inside (Diagram 4, next page); press. Topstitch around tab, ¼ inch from outer edge.

5. Center and sew the Velcro to tab lining side, ¼ inch from wide end (Diagram 5).

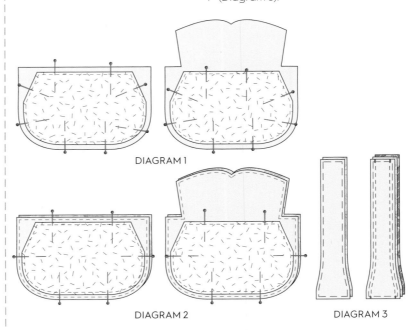

DIAGRAM 1

DIAGRAM 2

DIAGRAM 3

DIAGRAM 4

DIAGRAM 5

DIAGRAM 6

6. Fold clutch back in half lengthwise and finger-press a crease for a placement line. Unfold clutch back.

7. Mark a placement line 3½ inches above lower edge of clutch back on right side (Diagram 6). With right sides together, center narrow end of tab over center crease along marked placement line. Backstitching at the beginning and end, edgestitch across narrow end, then again ½ inch from edgestitching.

8. Fold tab over clutch back (Diagram 7, opposite). With 1 inch of tab extending toward bottom of bag, fold tab back on itself and up, centering it over center crease. Press and pin. The wide edge of the tab will extend past upper edge. Mark and sew across tab 5½ inches above bottom folded edge, backstitching at each edge to make a handle on clutch back; press.

ASSEMBLE CLUTCH

1. Fold clutch front in half widthwise and finger-press a crease for a placement line. Unfold clutch front.

2. Mark a placement line on clutch front 5 inches below upper edge at center fold (Diagram 8). Center and edgestitch loop portion of hook-and-loop tape to clutch front right side, just below marked line.

3. With the right sides together, align side and lower edges of clutch front and clutch back; pin. Using a ½-inch seam allowance, sew together along the side and lower edges (Diagram 9, opposite).

4. Trim seam allowance around bottom curves to ¼ inch. Press seam open using a pressing ham if desired. Turn right side out; press. **Note:** Pressing the seam open creates a crisp, finished look around curves at clutch bottom.

5. Repeat Steps 3 and 4 with coordinating print (lining) A and B pieces to make clutch lining.

6. With right side of clutch body facing in and wrong side of clutch lining facing out, place clutch body inside clutch lining, aligning side seams

(Diagram 10). Pin together raw edges, making sure tab is tucked in between clutch body and lining, out of the way. Using a ½-inch seam allowance, sew together raw edges, leaving a 5-inch opening for turning in center front.

7. Trim seam allowance across points of clutch back, making sure not to clip into stitching. Referring to Diagram 11, clip into seam allowance just to stitching line at corners where bag flap extends from clutch back. Clip into seam allowance at center top of clutch back.

8. Turn clutch right side out through 5-inch opening. Push lining down inside clutch, aligning side seams; press upper edges. To close opening, topstitch ⅛ inch from open edges of clutch (Diagram 12).

FINISH CLUTCH

1. On one side, match side seams on clutch body with lining; pin. With clutch body facing up, start at top finished edge on side seam and stitch in the ditch 3½ inches down (Diagram 13). Repeat on other side of clutch body.

2. To give the clutch shape, fold a 1¼-inch angled pleat into one side seam, beginning at the top and tapering pleat to end 3½ inches down (Diagram 14). Press folds in place. Repeat on remaining side seam. **Note:** The absence of ultra heavyweight interfacing in the area you're pleating should enable you to make crisp folds.

3. Attach a vintage pin onto right side of tab's wide end, covering stitching where Velcro was sewn.

4. Fold clutch back over clutch front, aligning Velcro closures, to complete the clutch.

DIAGRAM 7

DIAGRAM 8

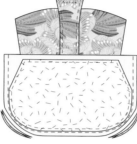

DIAGRAM 9

DIAGRAM 10

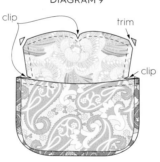

DIAGRAM 11

DIAGRAM 12

DIAGRAM 13

DIAGRAM 14

050
quilt a quick bag

Quilt, cut, sew, and go: Three fabrics, a few hours, and voilà—you'll have a fabulous purse!

YOU WILL NEED (for one bag)

⅝ yard large floral (outer bag body, handles, ties)

Scrap of small floral (gathering detail)

⅜ yard red batik (binding)

⅔ yard multicolor batik (inner bag body, handles)

24×42-inch thin cotton batting

Quilt basting spray (optional)

Finished Bag: Approximately 18 inches wide

Yardages and cutting instructions are based on 42 inches of usable fabric width.

Measurements include ¼-inch seam allowances unless otherwise indicated. Sew with right sides together unless otherwise indicated.

The Bag Body Pattern is in two parts (A and B) on Pattern Page I.

CUT THE PIECES:

From large floral, carefully trim off only 1 inch of each selvage edge, cutting:

2—1×18-inch strips (Set aside remaining large floral.)

From small floral, cut:

2—1¼×6½-inch rectangles

From red batik, cut:

Enough 1½-inch-wide bias strips to total 130 inches in length for binding (For details, see Cutting on the Bias in #093.)

QUILT AND CUT BAG PIECES

1. Lay ⅔-yard multicolor batik piece (approximately 24×42 inches) right side down on a flat surface. Center 24×42-inch batting rectangle on top. Center large floral rectangle (approximately 22½×40 inches) right side up on batting; baste layers. Or join the layers by spraying the wrong side of each fabric piece with quilt basting spray.

2. Quilt as desired to make a quilted rectangle. Quilting pattern options are shown in Diagrams 1–3 below.

3. To make a full pattern, trace both parts on a large sheet of paper, overlapping shaded areas.

Referring to Diagram 4, next page, from quilted rectangle, cut:

2 of Bag Body Pattern

2—2½×16-inch strips

ASSEMBLE BAG BODY AND ADD HANDLES

1. Press under ¼ inch on each edge of small floral 1¼×6½-inch rectangles. Referring to Bag Body Pattern and Diagram 5, next page, position a small floral rectangle on large floral side of a quilted bag body piece. Topstitch along long edges only. In the same manner, add remaining ➲

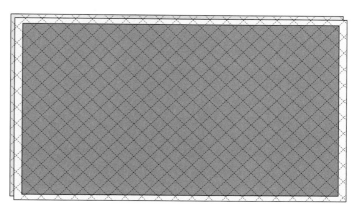

DIAGRAM 1

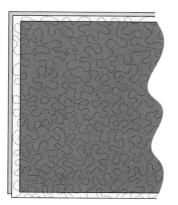

DIAGRAM 2

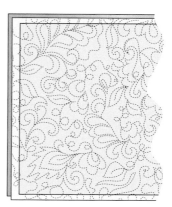

DIAGRAM 3

⟳ small floral 1¼×6½-inch rectangle to remaining bag body piece.

2. Referring to Bag Body Pattern, machine-sew with long stitches ⅛ inch from lower curved edge of a quilted bag body piece as marked. Leave long thread tails and do not backstitch (Diagram 6).

3. Pull thread tails to gather each lower curved edge of quilted bag body piece to about 4⅜ inches.

4. Repeat Steps 2 and 3 with remaining quilted bag body piece.

5. With right sides together, sew short ends of a quilted 2½×16-inch strip to a quilted bag body piece as a handle (Diagram 7). Press seams open. Repeat with remaining quilted 2½×16-inch strip and bag body piece.

6. With right sides together, align bottom curved edges of bag body pieces; pin. Sew together the side and bottom edges using a ¼-inch seam allowance to make bag body. Do not turn right side out.

BIND EDGES AND FINISH BAG

1. Sew together red batik 1½-inch-wide bias strips to make one long binding strip.

2. Using red batik binding strip and a scant ⅜-inch seam allowance, bind side and bottom edges of bag body using a single-fold method (Diagram 8). To apply a single-fold binding, follow instructions in #094, but do not fold binding strip in half lengthwise. Fold raw edge under a scant ⅜ inch before hand-stitching binding to backing.

3. Using remaining red batik binding strip, bind the four curves on top edges of bag body with single-fold binding (Diagram 9).

4. With wrong sides together, align long raw edges of a handle strip. Beginning and ending stitching ⅜ inch below the seam joining handle to bag body, sew together handle edges with a scant ⅜-inch seam allowance (Diagram 10). Using remaining red batik binding strip, bind handle raw edges, turning under ends of binding strip ⅜ inch at beginning and end. Turn bag body right side out.

5. Fold each large floral selvage 1×18-inch strip in half lengthwise with wrong side inside. Topstitch close to long raw edges to make two ties.

6. Thread a tie through the small floral rectangle on each side of outer bag body. Pull tie ends to gather; tie in overhand knots to complete bag.

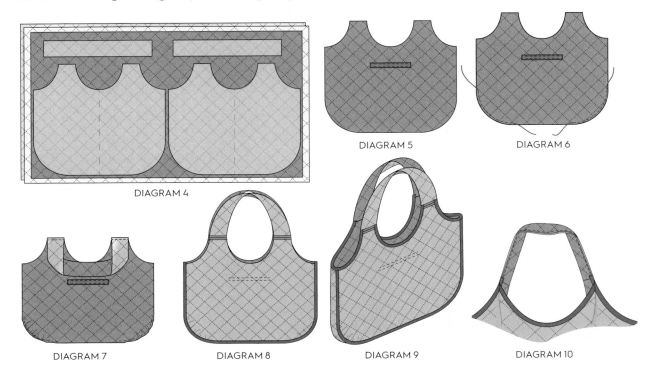

DIAGRAM 4

DIAGRAM 5

DIAGRAM 6

DIAGRAM 7

DIAGRAM 8

DIAGRAM 9

DIAGRAM 10

—Make in Minutes—

Embroider your initial with pretty hand-dyed ombré floss, then turn it into a custom charm with a modern metal pendant.

051
write a letter pendant

YOU WILL NEED

Rectangular necklace pendant (the pendant shown has a ⅞×1⅞-inch opening)

Scraps of cotton fabric: lavender and aqua

Embroidery needle*, thread, variegated embroidery floss

Water-soluble marking pen

Crafts glue and small paintbrush

Bead chain and clasp

1. Measure the pendant opening. Using an embroidery needle and thread, stitch a long running stitch onto the fabric to the same dimensions as the pendant opening.

Note: The stitches will be used as a guide for centering the embroidery and will be removed later.

2. Trace a letter from Pattern Page E onto fabric to fit inside your pendant using water-soluble marking pen.

3. Use three strands of embroidery floss for all stitches. Embroider the letters with small backstitches. For stitch diagrams and instructions, see #092.

4. When embroidery is complete, trim design to pendant dimensions, cutting through running-stitch lines; remove stitches.

5. Use a small paintbrush to coat the inside of the necklace pendant with

a thin layer of glue. Lightly press the finished embroidery inside the pendant.

6. Thread the bead chain through the pendant loop. Fasten the chain ends using a bead chain clasp.

*****Note:** Choose an embroidery needle that has a large enough eye to accommodate the type of thread you are working with and that is the proper size for the surface you are stitching on.

052
bag your brushes

It's time to face your cosmetics clutter. Corral your makeup brushes inside this clever roll-up pouch that has divided pockets to fit narrow and wide brushes. Then roll it up and fasten the tie ends for compact storage.

YOU WILL NEED

9×22-inch piece blue dot (pocket)

9×22-inch piece (fat eighth) teal dot (cover)

18×22-inch piece (fat quarter) green print (lining, tie, and binding)

8×12½-inch batting

Water- or air-soluble marking pen

Finished Brush Roll: 8×12½ inches

Fabrics are 44/45 inches wide. Sew with ¼-inch seam allowances and right sides together.

CUT THE PIECES:

From blue dot, cut:

1—7½×12½-inch pocket rectangle

From teal dot, cut:

1—8×12½-inch cover rectangle

From green print, cut:

1—8×12½-inch lining rectangle
2—1½×22-inch strips for tie
2—2½×22-inch binding strips

1. With wrong side inside, fold and press blue dot 7½×12½-inch rectangle in half lengthwise to make a 3¾×12½-inch pocket rectangle.

2. Layer teal dot 8×12½-inch cover rectangle wrong side up, 8×12½-inch batting rectangle, green print 8×12½-inch lining rectangle right side up, and pocket rectangle (Diagram 1). Pin layers together.

3. Mark stitching lines using a water- or air-soluble marking pen. Quilt layered roll with straight-stitch lines beginning 1¼ inches from a short edge (Diagram 2). Referring to diagram, continue quilting straight lines at 1- or 2-inch-wide intervals across surface of roll. Leave 1¼ inches unquilted along opposite short edge.

4. Join green print 1½×22-inch strips along one short edge; press seam open. With wrong side inside, fold and press green print 1½×43½-inch strip in half lengthwise. Open strip and press long edges to center fold line. Topstitch ⅛ inch from folded edges to make tie. Knot each end of tie and trim excess fabric at an angle to prevent raveling.

5. Fold tie in half. Pin center of tie to lining side of roll, aligning tie with folded top edge of pocket, to complete roll (Diagram 3).

6. Join short ends of binding strips. Press seam open. Fold in half lengthwise to make 1¼ inch double-fold binding. Aligning raw edges, join binding to brush roll cover using machine, keeping tie ends free from stitching. Turn folded edge of binding to brush roll lining and top-stitch edge of binding. (For details, see #094.)

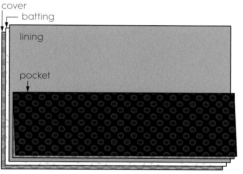

DIAGRAM 1

DIAGRAM 3

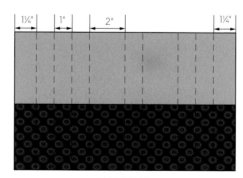

DIAGRAM 2

053
wrap up a scarf

Scarves have become anytime accessories. With stripes on one side and a solid on the other, the stripes act as a guide to add large running-stitch accents along the length of the scarf.

YOU WILL NEED

1 yard red stripe fabric*

¾ yard woven cotton linen

Size 5 embroidery needle

Valdani perle cotton: size 8 (M43–variegated multicolor reds)

*Note: Because the stripe on our fabric ran parallel to the selvage, extra yardage was required to allow for only one seam. If not using a directional or stripe fabric, you could buy only ¾ yard.

Finished Scarf: 63½×12½ inches

Measurements include ¼-inch seam allowances unless otherwise indicated. Sew with right sides together unless otherwise indicated.

CUT THE PIECES.

From each fabric, cut:

2—13×32-inch rectangles, noting direction of stripes (along 32-inch length).

1. With right sides together, sew ¼-inch seam along one short end of red stripe rectangle to make one long strip that is 13×63½ inches. Press seams open.

2. Repeat Step 1 for woven cotton linen rectangles.

3. Layer red stripe strip and woven cotton linen strip with right sides together. Sew ¼-inch seam on each long edge. Leave short ends unstitched. Turn right side out and

press. If you like, place pins along some of the red stripes to keep layers together while hand sewing.

4. Using a size 5 embroidery needle, thread approximately 18 inches of perle cotton and tie a knot. Starting on the red stripe fabric side of scarf, about ½ inch from end, stitch with a long running stitch along a stripe.

When you run out of thread, finish with a knot on the red strip side and begin again with another length of perle cotton.

5. Repeat Step 1 to sew along as many stripes as you want.

6. Pull out a few threads on each unfinished edge to create a frayed to finish.

054
put a bird on it

Use fusible web to adhere the fabric shapes to the shirt; then outline everything with big running stitches.

YOU WILL NEED

Tracing materials

Medium-weight fusible web (such as Steam-A-Seam)

8×16-inch piece of taupe print (branch)

5×8-inch piece of light blue print (bird)

Fabric scraps: lime green print (leaves) and dark blue print (wing)

Cotton T-shirt

Embroidery floss: taupe

1. Trace patterns (right) onto white paper; enlarge. Trace bird, wing, branch, and seven leaves onto paper side of fusible web, leaving 1-inch space between shapes. Cut out around shapes.

2. With fusible side down, press shapes onto wrong side of corresponding fabrics. Cut out shapes on the lines.

3. Place branch on left-hand side of T-shirt front, positioning left end of branch approximately 6½ inches below armhole opening and approximately ¼ inch from side seam. Referring to the Appliqué Placement Diagram, arrange bird, wing, and leaf shapes, overlapping pieces as shown. Press pieces.

4. Using two strands of taupe embroidery floss and a running stitch, outline the design approximately ¼ inch outside the shapes. See #092 for stitch diagrams and instructions.

APPLIQUÉ PLACEMENT DIAGRAM

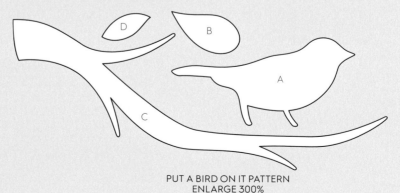

PUT A BIRD ON IT PATTERN
ENLARGE 300%

055
grow a garden apron

Make a garden apron using blue-and-white ticking and basic sewing skills. This design will hold a few tools in its roomy pockets.

YOU WILL NEED
Kraft paper or newsprint
½ yard cotton muslin
1 yard cotton ticking
Tape measure
76 inches twill tape
Sewing thread
Straight pins

1. Measure and cut 9×16-inch (pocket) and 18×27 inch (body) pattern pieces from kraft paper or newsprint. Pin patterns to fabric and cut out: ticking for the apron body and muslin for the pocket (A).

2. Set iron on medium-high/cotton setting. Prepare to hem apron body: Fold ½ inch of raw edges; pin as needed, press, remove pins. Fold another ½ inch on both sides and bottom; pin as needed; press. Fold another ¾ inch on top; pin; press (B).

3. Cut twill tape into two 38-inch-long pieces for the apron ties. Tuck one end of each tie under each end of the top hem, placing it ¾ inch in from apron side. Holding top hem in place over twill tape, pin tape between the layers of fabric (C).

4. Machine-stitch all the way around apron body ¼ inch from edge, then again ³/₈-inch from edge. Double stitching reinforces the apron so it will hold up to garden chores and multiple washings (D).

5. Hem pocket by folding ½ inch of both sides and bottom; pin, press, and remove pins. Fold the top 1 inch, pin, press, remove pins; fold another 1 inch, pin, press, and remove pins. Sew along top, stitching ¼ and ¾ inch from edge. For pocket placement: Fold apron and pocket in half, marking the center of each with pen. Place pocket so top is about 4 inches from top edge of apron, matching center marks; pin. Stitch sides and bottom ¼ inch from edge (E).

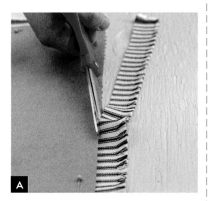
A

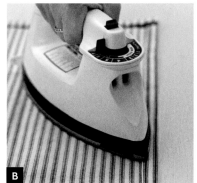
B

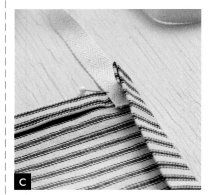
C

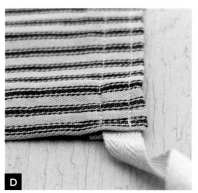
D

E

056
sew a small bag

Try this envelope bag as a clutch or as an insert in a larger bag.

YOU WILL NEED

12×21½-inch rectangle of turquoise print

12×21½-inch rectangle of black-and-white dot (for lining)

12×21½-inch rectangle of low-loft cotton batting

Matching thread

Set of sew-on Velcro dots

Button (optional)

1. Layer the turquoise print rectangle and the black-and-white dot rectangle with right sides together. Place them atop the batting rectangle with all edges aligned (Diagram 1).

2. Referring to Diagram 2, fold in the corners at one short end until they meet in the middle (as if starting a paper airplane). Press the folds with an iron to crease the fabrics.

3. Unfold the pressed corners and cut through all layers on the pressed lines (Diagram 3) to make the deconstructed envelope shape.

4. Referring to Diagram 4 and using a ½-inch seam allowance, sew around the deconstructed envelope, leaving a 4-inch opening along the bottom edge. To make it easier to keep the raw edges even, you may want to pin the layers together before beginning to sew. Sew with the batting on the bottom against the machine bed to prevent layers from shifting.

5. Turn the deconstructed envelope right side out through the opening. Use a pencil eraser or chopstick to push the corner points out smoothly. Press, turning the seam allowance at the unsewn opening under ½ inch so the bottom edge is straight.

6. Machine-stitch across the bottom edge using a wide zigzag stitch, making sure the right-hand swing of the needle goes just off the edge of the fabric (see photo, right). You will be stitching through three layers at this point.

7. With the point at the top and the lining fabric facing up, fold the bottom edge up 7 inches to form an envelope pocket. Pin each side edge, making sure the top edge is straight.

8. Backstitching at the beginning and ending of each seam, zigzag-stitch each 7-inch turned-up edge (Diagram 5). Again, make sure the right-hand swing of the needle goes just off the right-hand edge of the fabric (see photo, below). You'll be stitching through six layers at this point.

9. Fold the pointed flap over to make the envelope clutch. Position the Velcro dot closure in the desired position and hand-stitch in place to secure.

10. If desired, sew a button to the outside of the flap as a faux closure.

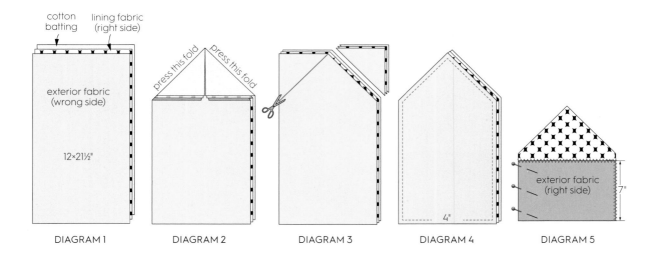

DIAGRAM 1   DIAGRAM 2   DIAGRAM 3   DIAGRAM 4   DIAGRAM 5

For Kids & Pets

Sew sweet blankets, toys, and lovies for the little ones for a special occasion, to mark a holiday, or just because. And don't forget your furry friends!

057
make a quick quilt

Ever wish you could just make a big Log Cabin block and be done with a quilt? Here it is—a fast, easy, and oh-so-versatile one-block quilt.

YOU WILL NEED

3½ yards total assorted polka dots in cream, blue, yellow, green, and red (block)

½ yard black-and-cream polka dot (binding)

3⅓ yards backing fabric (see About the Fabrics, below)

60-inch square batting

Finished Quilt: 51½-inch square

Quantities are for 44/45-inch-wide fabrics.

Measurements include ¼-inch seam allowances unless otherwise indicated. Sew with right sides together unless otherwise indicated.

ABOUT THE FABRICS

Bright polka dots of all sizes and colors make this quilt a hit with little ones. The common link among the fabrics is the cream background or polka dots.

For an oh-so-soft quilt, use plush fabric for the backing. Most plush fabrics are 59 inches wide, so if you choose it, you'll need just 1⅔ yards for the backing.

CUT THE PIECES

From assorted polka dots, cut:

2—7½×42-inch strips, cutting and piecing them to make one 7½×45½-inch rectangle for Position 15

2—6½×42-inch strips, cutting and piecing them to make one 6½×51½-inch rectangle for Position 16

2—6½×42-inch strips, cutting and piecing them to make one 6½×44½-inch rectangle for Position 14

1—8×38½-inch rectangle for Position 12
1—8×32-inch rectangle for Position 11
1—7×15½-inch rectangle for Position 5
1—6½×39½-inch rectangle for Position 13
1—6½×31-inch rectangle for Position 10
1—6½×21-inch rectangle for Position 6
1—6×26-inch rectangle for Position 9
1—6×14½-inch rectangle for Position 4
1—6×7-inch rectangle for block center
1—5×25½-inch rectangle for Position 8
1—5×21½-inch rectangle for Position 7
1—5×10-inch rectangle for Position 3
1—4½×10-inch rectangle for Position 2
1—3½×6-inch rectangle for Position 1

From black-and-cream polka dot, cut:

6—2½×42-inch binding strips

ASSEMBLE QUILT TOP

1. Sew assorted polka dot Position 1 rectangle to top edge of assorted polka dot 6×7-inch block center (Diagram 1). Press seam away from block center.

2. Add assorted polka dot Position 2 rectangle to left-hand edge of Step 1 unit (Diagram 2). Press seam as before.

3. Add assorted polka dot Position 3 rectangle to bottom edge of Step 2 unit; press as before (Diagram 3).

4. Referring to Quilt Assembly Diagram, continue sewing rectangles in a counterclockwise direction to make a Log Cabin block. Press all seams away from block center. The block, or quilt top, should be 51½-inch square including seam allowances.

FINISH QUILT

1. Layer quilt top, batting, and backing; baste. (For details, see #093.)

2. Quilt as desired. You can loop a meandering design across the quilt top to continue the polka dot theme as shown opposite.

3. Bind with black-and-cream polka dot binding strips. (For details, see #094.)

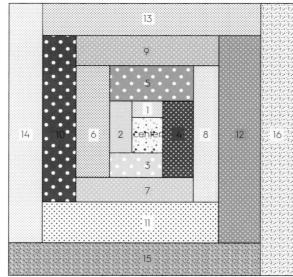

QUILT ASSEMBLY DIAGRAM

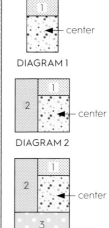

DIAGRAM 1

DIAGRAM 2

DIAGRAM 3

058
sprout a little quilt

An easy appliqué method makes the leaves on this kid-friendly quilt spring to life in no time—we promise!

YOU WILL NEED

Tracing marker

220-grit sandpaper

1⅔ yards solid white (appliqué foundations, outer border)

1½ yards green print (sashing, appliqués, inner border, binding)

¾ yard sheer, featherweight, nonfusible, nonwoven interfacing

3 yards backing fabric

54-inch square batting

Finished Quilt: 46×45½ inches

Quantities are for 44/45-inch-wide, 100% cotton fabrics.

Measurements include ¼-inch seam allowances unless otherwise indicated. Sew with right sides together unless otherwise indicated.

The leaf pattern is on Pattern Page A. To make a template of the pattern, see #093.

CUT THE PIECES

From solid white, cut:
5—3×42-inch strips for outer border
4—9×38½-inch appliqué foundation strips

From green print, cut:
5—2½×42-inch binding strips
3—2×38½-inch sashing strips
2—1½×41-inch inner border strips
2—1½×38½-inch inner border strips
28—4½×6½-inch rectangles for appliqués

From interfacing, cut:
28—4½×6½-inch rectangles for appliqués

ASSEMBLE QUILT CENTER

Referring to Quilt Assembly Diagram (next page), sew together solid white 9×38½-inch appliqué foundation strips and green print 2×38½-inch sashing strips to make quilt center. Press seams open. The quilt center should be 39×38½ inches including seam allowances.

PREPARE APPLIQUÉS

1. Use a tracing marker to trace leaf template onto wrong side of a green print 4½×6½-inch rectangle. (To prevent fabric from stretching as you draw lines, place 220-grit sandpaper under the rectangle.) The drawn line is the stitching line (Diagram 1, next page).

2. Layer marked rectangle atop a 4½×6½-inch interfacing rectangle, right sides together (Diagram 2, next page).

3. Sew pieces together, stitching on marked line. Cut out appliqué shape, adding a ³⁄₁₆-inch seam allowance (Diagram 3, next page).

4. Trim interfacing seam allowance slightly smaller than green print seam allowance. Trimming in this way enables seam allowance to roll slightly toward back side of appliqué once it is turned. Clip curved edge and point just up to stitching line (Diagram 4, next page).

5. Clip a small slit in center of interfacing, being careful not to cut through green print appliqué shape (Diagram 5, next page).

6. Turn appliqué piece right side out through slit (Diagram 6, next page).

7. Press appliqué piece from right side to make a leaf appliqué.

8. Repeat Steps 1 through 7 to make 28 leaf appliqués total.

APPLIQUÉ QUILT CENTER

1. Referring to photo on previous spread arrange prepared leaf appliqués along green print sashing strips in quilt center. Pin or baste appliqués in place.

2. Using thread in a color to match appliqués and a blind hemstitch, machine-appliqué pieces in place.

ADD BORDERS

1. Referring to Quilt Assembly Diagram, below, join green print 1½×38½-inch inner border strips to side edges of quilt center. Add green print 1½×41-inch inner border strips to remaining edges. Press all seams toward inner border.

2. Cut and piece solid white 3×42-inch strips to make two 3×46-inch outer border strips and two 3×40½-inch outer border strips.

3. Join short outer border strips to side edges of quilt center. Add long outer border strips to remaining edges to complete quilt top. Press all seams toward outer border.

FINISH QUILT

1. Layer quilt top, batting, and backing; baste. (For details, see #093.)

2. To quilt, stitch in the ditch around the green print sashing strips and inner border to secure the quilt top. Echo-quilt stylized leaves inside each

appliquéd leaf. (Echo-quilting is when you follow the shape of the appliqué design. It can be done with a free motion foot or a walking foot.) To finish, stitch circles in the solid white appliqué backgrounds and outer border.

3. Bind with green print binding strips. (For details, see #094.)

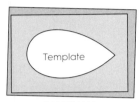

DIAGRAM 1

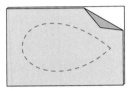

DIAGRAM 2

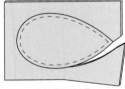

DIAGRAM 3

DIAGRAM 4

DIAGRAM 5

DIAGRAM 6

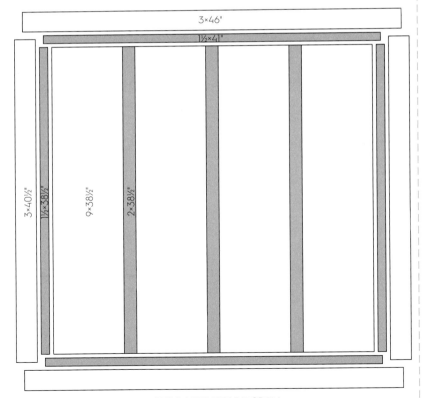

QUILT ASSEMBLY DIAGRAM

—Make in Minutes—

Contain spills, splatters, and drips from Fido's feeding frenzy with a laminated fabric mat that protects your floor from standing water and adds a decorative element in an unexpected place.

059
give a dog a bone

YOU WILL NEED
½ yard of cotton fabric
1 yard of Heat 'n' Bond Vinyl
Fine-tip permanent marking pen
Sewing machine
Matching sewing thread

1. Cut two 13×26-inch rectangles each from the fabric and the vinyl. (You will have four rectangles total.)

2. Adhere a vinyl rectangle to a fabric rectangle using an iron and following manufacturer's instructions. Repeat with remaining vinyl and fabric rectangles.

3. Enlarge the pattern, right, onto white paper; cut out. Trace the shape onto each vinyl-covered rectangle using a fine-tip permanent marking pen; cut out.

4. With vinyl sides facing each other, sew together the bone shapes using a ¼-inch seam allowance and leaving a 3-inch opening along one side.

5. Turn bone-shape mat right side out through the 3-inch opening. Turn under seam allowance at the opening and hand-stitch it closed. Topstitch with a ¼-inch seam allowance around the place mat edges.

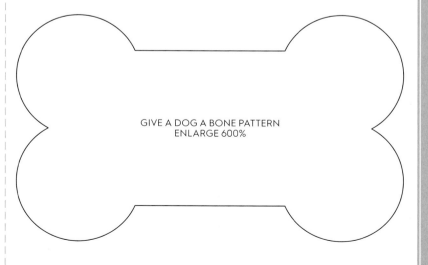

GIVE A DOG A BONE PATTERN
ENLARGE 600%

O6O
make a modern baby quilt

Improv piecing, adorable elephants, and a mix of prints and solids make for baby room décor with a modern edge.

YOU WILL NEED

1 yard solid gray fabric

1⅛ yards blue-green stripe fabric

¼ yard each of 6 to 10 coordinating fabrics

1⅝ yards of backing fabric

44×56-inch quilt batting

Rotary cutter, ruler, and mat

Finished Quilt: 36×48 inches

Fabrics are 44/45 inches wide. Sew with ¼-inch seam allowances and right sides together.

CUT THE PIECES

From solid gray, cut:

1—5×42-inch strip

4—2½×36½-inch strips

5—2½×42-inch binding strips

From blue-green stripe (cut so the stripes are vertical on the quilt):

1—36½×18½-inch rectangle

6—1½×36½-inch strips

From each coordinating fabric, cut:

1—5×42-inch strip

1. Stack solid gray and assorted 5×42-inch strips on cutting mat with right sides up and long edges aligned. Using rotary cutter and acrylic ruler, press firmly on stack and make a series of random angled cuts about 4 inches apart along entire strip (Diagram 1). (For this quilt, 11 cuts were made, yielding 12 stacks of fabric.) Leave stacks in place.

2. Create four pieced rows from the stacks. Take top fabric from Stack 1 and place it in a second row, directly below first (Diagram 2, opposite). Keeping stacks in place, choose a fabric from Stack 2 and move it into second row. Continue until a piece from each stack has been used.

3. Sew together pieces in Row 2 in order. Press all seams in one direction. Long edges of strip will be slightly uneven. Trim pieced strip to measure 4½×36 inches.

4. Repeat Steps 2 and 3 to make four pieced strips total.

5. Referring to Quilt Assembly Diagram, sew together strips to make quilt top. Press all seams toward lower edge.

6. Layer quilt top, batting, and backing; baste. Quilt as desired. The quilt pictured was stitched in the ditch across all seams and machine-

stitched with straight lines running horizontally on solid gray strips and vertically on green stripe rectangle. On pieced strips, straight lines were stitched ½ inch on either side of each seam. If you prefer to hand-quilt, use three strands of embroidery floss and big stitches, each about ¼ inch long.

7. Join short ends of binding strips. Press seams open. Fold in half lengthwise to make 1¼-inch double-fold binding. Aligning raw edges, join binding to quilt top by machine. Turn folded edge of binding to quilt back and hand-stitch in place. (For details, see #094.)

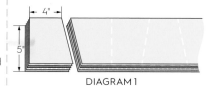

DIAGRAM 1

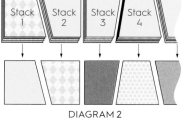

DIAGRAM 2

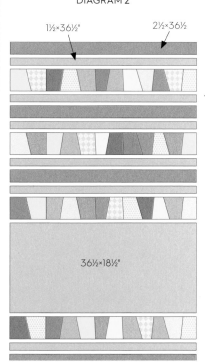

1½×36½"   2½×36½"

36½×18½"

QUILT ASSEMBLY DIAGRAM

061
mobilize an elephant parade

This sweet circus mobile is a perfect handmade addition to a nursery. It's for decoration only, is not a toy, and should be kept out of reach of young children and infants because it contains small parts.

YOU WILL NEED

Lightweight fusible web (such as Steam-A-Seam)

12×18-inch wool-blend felt in blue

9×12-inch wool-blend felt in teal, yellow, gold, orange, white, gray, pink

Cotton polka-dot fabric scraps in assorted colors to match

Polyester fiberfill

Heavyweight thread (such as hand-quilting thread)

Embroidery floss: black, orange

Yarn

Narrow masking tape

9-inch-diameter wood embroidery hoop (you'll use only the inner hoop)

8—2-cm felt balls in assorted matching colors

Chopstick (optional)

Patterns are on Pattern Page J.

MAKE ELEPHANTS

1. Trace Inner Ear pattern onto paper side of fusible web eight times, leaving ½ inch between tracings. Cut out each fusible-web shape roughly ¼ inch outside traced lines. Following manufacturer's instructions, press fusible-web shapes onto backs of assorted fabric scraps in matching pairs; cool. Cut out fabric shapes on drawn lines; peel off paper backings.

2. Referring to photo for color placement, cut following pieces for each elephant from assorted felt:

2 each of Body, Saddle, Outer Ear, Star, and Cheek patterns

Cut 4—1⅛×18-inch matching strips of felt to cover hoop and set aside.

3. Referring to photo, arrange matching Inner Ear pieces to matching Outer Ear pieces. Following manufacturer's instructions and using a press cloth between felt and iron, fuse shapes in place with hot iron. Zigzag-stitch around curved edge of each Inner Ear to secure.

4. Place two Body pieces that match Step 3 Outer Ears on table with trunks facing (so they are mirror images). Place matching Saddles in position on each Elephant. Using matching thread, edgestitch saddles in place along curved lower edge only (Diagram 1). Do not sew top curve of saddle.

5. With matching threads, edgestitch a Star onto far side of saddle (away from head) and Cheek near trunk. Repeat for opposite side of elephant.

6. Place fused ear on Elephant and attach by zigzag-stitching only the straight edge to create a dimensional ear. Hand-sew a double-wrap French knot for elephant eye. Repeat for opposite side of elephant.

7. With wrong sides together, pin elephant bodies together, then sew around ⅛ inch from outer edge with contrasting thread, leaving a 1-inch opening.

8. Stuff elephant lightly with polyester fiberfill through opening. Use a chopstick to help push stuffing into narrow trunk and leg areas. Stitch opening closed in the same manner as before.

9. Repeat Steps 3 through 8 to make four elephants total.

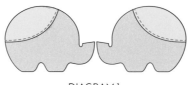

DIAGRAM 1

10"

DIAGRAM 2

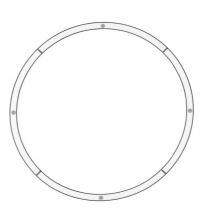

DIAGRAM 3

MAKE BALANCING BALLS

1. Referring to photo, on previous page, for color placement, cut the following pieces for two balancing balls from assorted felt:

4 each of Ball, Stripes, and Tip patterns (in two matching sets of two colors each)

2. Place Stripes piece atop Ball piece. Using matching thread, edgestitch Stripes in place. Position matching Tip piece over center intersection of Ball Stripes and edgestitch in place. Trim any excess felt overhanging edges to make one balancing ball. Repeat to make a second matching balancing ball.

3. With wrong sides together, pin the balancing balls; then sew around ⅛ inch from outer edge, leaving a 1-inch opening. Stuff ball lightly with polyester fiberfill. Stitch opening closed.

4. Repeat to make a second balancing ball.

MAKE BUNTING

1. Referring to the photo for color placement, cut the following pieces to make four bunting strips from assorted felt:
24 of Bunting Pattern
1 of Flag Pattern

2. Align short edges of six assorted Bunting pieces. Leaving needle and bobbin threads at least 10 inches long, sew across short edges of triangles, very close to edge, allowing needle to sew a couple of stitches between each triangle to make a bunting strip (Diagram 2, previous page). Leave needle and bobbin threads 10 inches long before cutting bunting strip from machine. Repeat to make a total of four bunting strips.

ASSEMBLE MOBILE

1. Measure and, using a pencil, mark four lines on top edge of embroidery hoop (inner hoop only), evenly spaced around hoop. Then mark four dots, evenly spaced between drawn lines (Diagram 3, previous page).

2. Wrap one end of a 34-inch length of yarn to hoop on one line; secure with tape in place on inside and outside of hoop. Wrap other end of yarn on line on opposite side and tape in place. Repeat with a second length of yarn on remaining two lines.

3. Place hoop on a flat surface, hold two pieces of yarn centered and taut above hoop, and tie a knot 6 inches from top. Fold Flag piece in half around yarn above knot and edgestitch along raw edges (Diagram 4). Tie a second knot just above flag.

4. Hang embroidery hoop from top yarn loops. Referring to photo for placement and using heavy thread and a hand-sewing needle, create two 18-inch-long strings, each with an elephant and a balancing ball. Upper and lower strings should attach to elephant at hanger positions marked on pattern piece. Create a second set and two long strings holding elephants and threaded felt balls. Make sure strings are evenly weighted. For maximum visibility, position elephants at different heights.

5. Tie four strings of elephants at marked dots (on ours, strings are 12 and 14 inches long below hoop); secure with tape, making sure hoop is balanced so it hangs straight.

6. Attach four bunting strings so they drape between strings of elephants with flags on each end approximately ¼ inch below hoop, tying them at same points as elephants, and secure with tape.

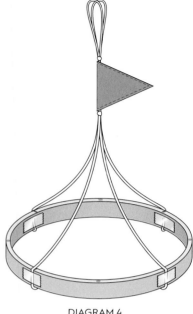

DIAGRAM 4

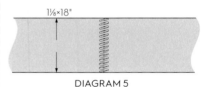

1⅛×18"

DIAGRAM 5

7. Using matching thread, abut short ends of two 1⅛×18-inch strips and sew together with a zigzag stitch to make one long strip that lies flat (Diagram 5). Wrap felt strip around outside of hoop and trim to size, again abutting raw ends. Remove remaining felt zigzag short ends together to make a loop. Repeat with remaining two felt strips, measuring inside of hoop.

8. Place felt loops on inside and outside of hoop, then hand-stitch together with five strands of orange embroidery floss around top and bottom, using a running stitch ⅛ inch from edges to complete mobile.

062
stitch a stuffed animal

Watch imaginations soar as kids play with these oversize plush toys.

YOU WILL NEED

FOR THE FISH

Tracing paper; pencil

½ yard dot fleece

¼ yard fleece in red, green, orange

Felt scraps in green, black, red

Sewing machine and matching threads

Hand-sewing needle

Embroidery floss; yellow, black

Polyester batting

FOR THE BIRD

Tracing paper; pencil

½ yard fleece for body

¼ yard each fleece in contrasting colors for wings and tail loops

Scrap of orange felt for beak; scrap of dark green felt for eyes

Sewing machine and thread

2 small cabone rings

Black perle cotton

Crochet hook

Polyester batting

Hand-sewing needle

Narrow cording

FOR THE FISH

1. Trace pattern pieces on Pattern Page K; enlarge. Cut fleece according to patterns. Layer tail and fin pieces and topstitch together. Layer stripes on fish body and topstitch. Topstitch mouth and eye in place. Detail eye with straight stitches around eye and a French knot in eye center (see #092).

2. Pleat straight end of front side fins and topstitch to fish body. Stitch top and bottom fins and tail to body. With right sides facing, stitch body sides together,

leaving an opening for turning. Clip seams as necessary. Turn to right side.

3. Fill fish with batting. Stitch the opening closed.

FOR THE BIRD

1. Trace pattern pieces on Pattern Page K; enlarge. Cut fleece according to pattern pieces. Layer wing pieces and topstitch together. Topstitch wing pieces to body at placement on body side. Topstitch felt circle eye to body.

2. Work single crochet around cabone ring with black perle cotton. Hand-stitch cabone ring to felt eye. Topstitch beak pieces to body. With right sides facing, stitch gusset to each body piece and stitch body pieces together, leaving an opening

for turning and small opening to insert tail. Clip seam as necessary and turn to right side.

3. Fill bird with batting. Stitch the opening closed.

4. To make tail loops, cut 1-inch-wide fleece strips to desired length. With two times as much cording length as fleece strips, place cording lengthwise on right side of fleece. Stitch fleece lengthwise with a narrow seam, keeping cording free. Secure cording to fleece where extra cording is exposed. Turn fleece to right side over extra cording. Make loops for tail. Fold ends into loops to hide and secure to bird with hand stitches.

063
trim a tree with a birdie

These felt bird ornaments are all atwitter! Choose your favorite felt colors for their colored bellies and coil felt strips into dimensional flowers to customize them to your own style.

YOU WILL NEED (for one bird)

Felt: gray, white, orange, green, and colors of your choice for belly and flowers

Water-soluble marking pen

Sewing thread: white, orange, green, gray

Two black ⅛-inch-diameter brads

Polyester fiberfill

Hot-glue gun and glue sticks

CUT THE PIECES

From gray felt, cut:
2 of Pattern A (body)
1 of Pattern F (feathers)

From color of your choice, cut:
1 of Pattern B (belly)

From white felt, cut:
2 of Pattern C (eyes)

From orange felt, cut:
1 of Pattern D (beak)

From green felt, cut:
2 of Pattern E (leaves)

1. Referring to Appliqué Placement Diagram, pin belly to body front, approximately 1 inch below the top edge of the body; topstitch in place. Pin eyes on top half of body front, overlapping bottom ¼ inch of each eye on the top of the belly; topstitch in place. Topstitch beak between the eyes. Attach a brad to each eye through the felt layers, positioning each one slightly off center so the bird is looking to the side.

2. Place body front and body back pieces together with wrong sides facing and feathers sticking out of the top. Sew the pieces together using a ¼-inch seam allowance, leaving a 1-inch opening along the bottom edge. Firmly stuff the bird with polyester fiberfill through the opening. Hand-stitch the opening closed. Trim the seam allowance to ¹⁄₁₆ inch around the outside edges.

3. Cut a 1×12-inch strip from desired felt for flower. Fold the strip in half lengthwise and make ¼-inch-deep cuts into the folded edge. Space each cut ¼ inch apart along the length of the folded strip.

4. Glue the folded strip together along the long straight edges; do not glue the folded cut edge. Roll the strip tightly to make a flower, gluing the coil together as needed along the straight edges.

5. Referring to the photo, below, for placement, glue the leaves to the lower left-hand corner of the bird's belly. Hot-glue the flower on top of the leaves.

ENLARGE ALL 150%

D

C

E

F

SEND TWEETNESS PATTERN A
ENLARGE 150%

SEND TWEETNESS PATTERN B
ENLARGE 150%

F
A
C   C
D
B

APPLIQUÉ PLACEMENT DIAGRAM

064
make a forest friend

The only thing this squeezable raccoon will steal is your heart. Complete the 10-inch-tall plush with a fun embellished forest tree motif on his belly.

YOU WILL NEED

9×12-inch piece each of felt: gray, black, white

¼ sheet of white felt

Embroidery needle

Embroidery floss: white, gray, turquoise, dark brown, black

Crafts glue

Water-soluble marking pen

Polyester fiberfill

Finished Raccoon: about 7×10 inches

CUT THE PIECES

From gray felt, cut:
1 of Pattern A (front)

From black felt, cut:
1 of Pattern A (back)
2 of Pattern B (inner mask)
2 of Pattern C (paws)
1 of Pattern D (nose)
1 of Pattern E (tail stripe 1)
1 of Pattern F (tail stripe 2)
1 of Pattern G (tail stripe 3)

From white felt, cut:
2 of Pattern H (outer mask)
1 of Pattern I (belly)

Note: Appliqué pieces using a ⅛-inch seam allowance. See #092 for embroidery stitches diagrams and instructions.

1. Using three strands of white embroidery floss and referring to the pattern for placement, backstitch the outline of an eye onto each black inner mask piece. Fill in each eye outline using white satin stitches.

2. Using six strands of black embroidery floss wrapped three times around the needle, stitch a French knot pupil on top of each satin-stitched eye.

3. Using two strands of gray embroidery floss and running stitches, attach a black inner mask to a white outer mask piece. Repeat with remaining black inner mask and white outer mask pieces.

4. Referring to Appliqué Placement Diagram, opposite, position mask pieces, nose, paws, and tail stripes on gray body front. Pin or use small dots of crafts glue to hold pieces in place. Backstitch the pieces to the body front using two strands of gray embroidery floss.

5. Lay white felt belly piece on belly pattern and trace the tree onto the felt using a water-soluble marking pen. Using six strands of turquoise embroidery floss and split stitches, sew on the tree. Using six strands of brown embroidery floss wrapped three times around the needle, stitch a French knot at the end of each branch. Referring to the pattern for placement, backstitch the belly to the body front using two strands of gray embroidery floss.

6. Place the gray body front and the black body back pieces together with wrong sides facing. Using three strands of black embroidery floss, blanket-stitch the pieces together along the outside edges, leaving a 3-inch opening along the bottom edge for stuffing. Stuff the raccoon with polyester fiberfill, then finish blanket-stitching the edges together.

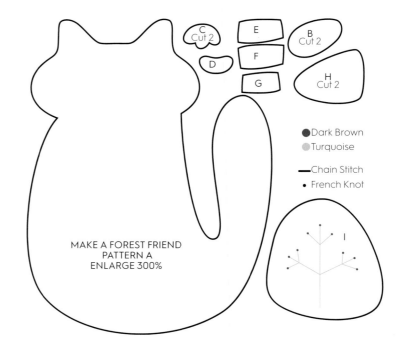

● Dark Brown
● Turquoise

— Chain Stitch
• French Knot

MAKE A FOREST FRIEND
PATTERN A
ENLARGE 300%

APPLIQUÉ PLACEMENT DIAGRAM

Stitch the fox's tail to the back of the bag!

065
make a foxy bag

Some consider the fox to be the master of trickery, and even this crafty felt fellow has a secret to hide. His appliquéd face grins from the flap of the child-size messenger bag, but turn the bag around and you'll reveal his bushy tail.

YOU WILL NEED

9×12-inch piece each of felt or wool felt: one cream, two orange, two turquoise

Scrap of black felt or wool felt

½ yard lining fabric

Matching sewing threads

White embroidery floss

Water-soluble marking pen

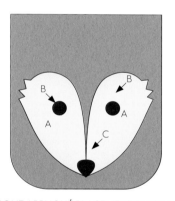

FRONT APPLIQUÉ PLACEMENT DIAGRAM

DIAGRAM 1

Finished Bag: about 8×10×2 inches

Measurements include ½-inch seam allowances unless otherwise indicated. Sew with right sides together unless otherwise indicated.

Patterns are on Pattern Page H.

CUT THE PIECES

From cream felt or wool felt, cut:
2 of Pattern A (eyes)
1 of Pattern E (tail tip)

From orange felt or wool felt, cut:
1 of Pattern D (tail)
1—8×9½-inch rectangle (flap)

From scrap of black felt or wool felt, cut:
2 of Pattern B (eyes)
1 of Pattern C (nose)

From lining fabric, cut:
2—10-inch squares (body lining)
1—8×9½-inch rectangle (flap lining)

From turquoise wool felt, cut:
1—4×32-inch strip (handle)
2—10-inch squares (bag exterior)

1. Referring to the Front Appliqué Placement Diagram, arrange the cream eye pieces on the orange felt flap; pin. Using matching thread, topstitch the pieces in place using a scant 1/16-inch seam allowance. Arrange the black eye and nose pieces on the eye pieces; hand-stitch in place using black sewing thread. Using white embroidery floss, stitch a small cross-stitch on each eye.

2. Use a cup and a water-soluble marking pen to mark rounded corners on bottom of orange flap and flap lining pieces; trim along the lines. With right sides together, sew the flap exterior and lining together using a ¼-inch seam allowance; leave the top open (Diagram 1). Turn right side out and press. Edgestitch around the sides and bottom.

3. Referring to the Back Appliqué Placement Diagram, arrange the orange tail piece and the cream tail tip piece on the right side of one turquoise 10-inch square. Overlap the tail tip slightly on the tail. Using matching thread, topstitch the pieces in place using a scant 1/16-inch seam allowance.

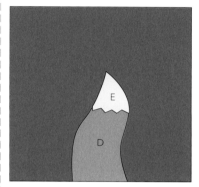

BACK APPLIQUÉ PLACEMENT DIAGRAM

DIAGRAM 2

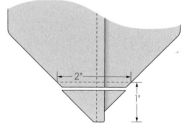

DIAGRAM 3

4. With right sides together, sew the turquoise 10-inch squares together by stitching down one side, across the bottom (the edge with the tail), and up the opposite side; leave the top edge open (Diagram 2, previous page).

5. To shape flat bottom for bag, at one corner match bottom seam line to side seam line, creating a flattened triangle (Diagram 3, previous page). Measuring 1 inch from point of triangle, draw a 2-inch-long line across triangle. Sew on drawn line. Trim excess fabric. Repeat with remaining bottom corner to make bag body. Turn right sides out.

6. With right sides together, sew the lining fabric 10-inch squares together along the sides and bottom; leave a 4-inch opening in the center of the bottom and the top edge open (Diagram 4).

7. Refer to the instructions in Step 5 to shape flat bottom for bag lining (Diagram 5).

8. Press under ½ inch along each long edge of the turquoise handle strip. Fold the handle strip in half and topstitch ¼ inch from folded edges to make the handle. Final handle width should measure 1½ inches (Diagram 6).

9. With right sides together, align the raw edges of the flap and the back of the bag body (the fox face should face the tail); pin and baste in place (Diagram 7).

10. Center the ends of the handle along the bag body sides, positioning the ends ¼ inch above the top of the side edge (Diagram 8). Baste the ends in place.

11. Insert bag body into bag lining with right sides together. Align the side seams and top raw edges. Tuck in and smooth down flap and strap. Pin and topstitch around top of bag, catching the handles in the seam (Diagram 9). Reinforce the handles.

12. Pull bag right side out through the lining opening. Using a small seam allowance, fold in raw edges and sew the lining closed. Smooth lining and press. Topstitch around top of bag using a ¼-inch seam allowance.

DIAGRAM 7

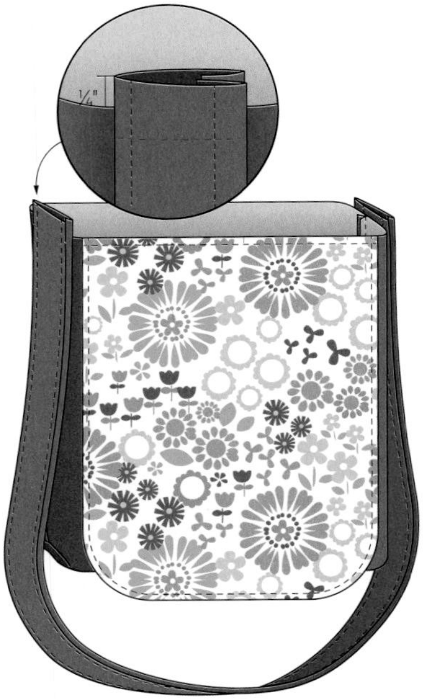

DIAGRAM 8

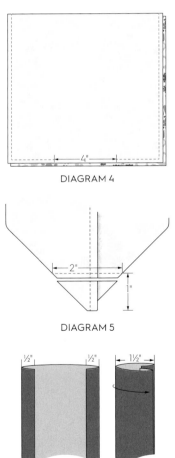

DIAGRAM 4

DIAGRAM 5

DIAGRAM 6

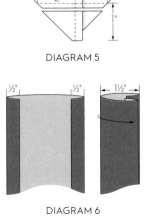

DIAGRAM 9

—Make in Minutes—

These sassy ninjas have something to hide: a tube of lip balm in their back pockets.
Make them by the dozen to share with friends.

066
craft secret storage

YOU WILL NEED (for one ninja)

5×10-inch rectangle of felt in desired color (for body)

Felt scraps in assorted colors (for face, belt, and flower)

Embroidery floss: black and colors to match body and belt

Two ¼-inch-diameter black buttons (for eyes)

Key ring

Patterns are on Pattern Page J.

CUT THE PIECES

From 5×10-inch felt rectangle, cut:
2 of Body Pattern

From felt scraps, cut:
1 each of Face, Belt, Flower, and Flower Center patterns
½×2-inch strip for key ring loop

1. Referring to Diagram 1, trace oval face opening from pattern onto one felt Body piece and cut away. On remaining Body piece, cut a slit as indicated on pattern for lip balm opening. Sew eyes onto Face.

2. Pin Face piece in place behind opening on front Body piece. Using two strands of floss matching Body, blanket-stitch Face in place. To blanket-stitch, pull needle up at A (Blanket Stitch Diagram), form a reverse L shape with floss, and hold angle of L shape in place with your thumb. Push needle down at B and come up at C to

secure stitch. Continue in same manner around entire opening.

3. In same manner, blanket-stitch Belt to Body front. Position Flower Center atop Flower. Use four straight stitches through all layers to secure flower center to belt center.

4. On Body Back, use two strands of matching floss to blanket-stitch around entire opening to finish raw edge (Diagram 2).

5. With wrong sides together, place two Body pieces atop one another; pin. Fold ½×2-inch strip in half around key ring to make a ½×1-inch key ring loop. Position raw edges of key ring loop ¼ inch below top of head and between body layers; pin (Diagram 3). Using two strands of matching floss, blanket-stitch around entire body to complete lip balm holder. Insert lip balm in back.

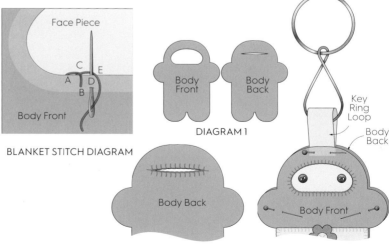

Face Piece

C E
A D
B

Body Front

BLANKET STITCH DIAGRAM

Body Front   Body Back

DIAGRAM 1

Body Back

DIAGRAM 2

Key Ring Loop

Body Back

Body Front

DIAGRAM 3

067
create a friendly monster

Craft a one-eyed creature to delight kids big and small.

YOU WILL NEED

Green sweater

Sweater or fabric scraps for eye, mouth, teeth, horns, and optional eyelashes

Zipper for mustache embellishment (optional)

Thin cotton batting

½ cup plastic stuffing pellets (for stand-up monster)

Funnel

Polyester fiberfill

If you want to make a flat monster, eliminate the base and use the curved line at the bottom of the Body Pattern on Pattern Page K. If you want a stand-up monster, use the straight line at the bottom of the Body Pattern. Also choose the green curved horns or the contrasting-color triangular ears and cut the appropriate pieces.

From green sweater, cut:

2 of Body Pattern
1 of Base Pattern
2 each of Horn Pattern and Horn Pattern reversed

From sweater and fabric scraps, cut:

1 each of Eye, Pupil, Mouth, Big Tooth, and Small Tooth patterns
1—1½×4-inch strip for eyelashes
4 of Ear Pattern

From batting, cut:

2 of Body Pattern
2 of Base Pattern

1. Referring to patterns on Pattern Page K and photo, left, position mouth, teeth, eye, and pupil shapes on one green sweater body piece as desired; pin in place. To add eyelashes, fold 1½×4-inch strip in half lengthwise and clip raw edges every ½ inch; tuck folded edge of strip beneath top edge of eye and pin before sewing along top edge of eye. Using a machine zigzag stitch, sew along edges of each piece to appliqué face.

2. Add desired embellishments, such as a zipper-teeth mustache.

3. If making horns: Layer a green sweater Horn and Horn reversed piece right sides together. Using ¼-inch seam allowance, sew along curved edges only (Diagram 1). Turn right side out and stuff lightly with fiberfill. Pin or baste opening closed. Repeat to make a second horn.

4. If making ears: Layer two fabric ear pieces right sides together. Using ¼-inch seam allowance, sew along two edges as shown (Diagram 2). Turn right side out and press flat. Fold a ¼-inch pleat in the bottom edge and pin or baste edges closed. Repeat to make a second ear.

5. With raw edges aligned, position horns or ears on right side of body piece with appliquéd face; baste in place (Diagram 3).

6. With sweater right side up, layer each sweater body atop a batting body piece. Baste layers together ¼ inch or less from all edges (or zigzag-stitch over raw edges).

7. For flat monster: With sweater right sides together, sew body pieces together along all edges, leaving a 2-inch opening on one side.

8. For stand-up monster: Place two batting base circles on wrong side of sweater base circle. Using a ½-inch seam allowance, sew through all layers, leaving a 1-inch opening, to form a pouch (Diagram 4). Use a funnel to insert plastic stuffing pellets into the pouch. Sew opening closed.

9. With sweater right sides together, sew body pieces together along all edges, leaving a 2-inch opening on one side (Diagram 5).

10. Using a ¼-inch seam, sew base pouch to bottom opening of the joined body pieces (Diagram 6).

11. Turn monster right side out through opening. Stuff monster with fiberfill. (Depending on the sweater you used for your body, the monster might stretch and get taller when you stuff it.) Sew the opening closed to complete monster.

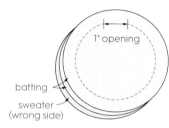

1" opening

batting

sweater (wrong side)

DIAGRAM 4

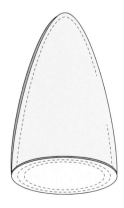

2" opening

DIAGRAM 5

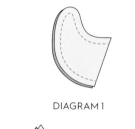

DIAGRAM 1

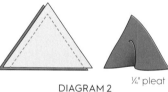

DIAGRAM 2

¼" pleat

DIAGRAM 3

DIAGRAM 6

068
store classic cars

There's plenty of parking for toy cars in a portable carport that's the perfect size for taking along.

YOU WILL NEED

17-inch square of denim (for outer shell and pocket)

17×10-inch rectangle of green cotton (for lining)

17×3-inch strip of gray felt (for road)

Scrap of yellow felt, blue felt, and gray polka-dot cotton (for road dashes, wheels, and car appliqué)

52 inches of premade ½-inch white, corded piping (such as Wrights)

1-inch square of sew-on Velcro

6-inch piece of 1-inch-wide cotton webbing

4-inch square of lightweight fusible web

2-inch-tall iron-on white numbers

Jeans/Denim sewing machine needle, size 70/10

Patterns are on Pattern Page H.

CUT THE PIECES

From denim, cut:
1—17×10-inch rectangle
1—17×7-inch strip

From yellow felt scrap, cut:
8—1×¼-inch strips

From blue felt scrap, cut:
2 of Wheel Pattern

1. With wrong sides inside, fold 17×7-inch denim strip in half to make a 17×3½-inch pocket strip; press. Aligning long raw edges, sew denim pocket strip to 17×10-inch lining (Diagram 1). Referring to Diagram 1 for spacing, sew vertical lines through all fabric layers to make pockets, backstitching at beginning and end of each line for added stability. Adhere iron-on numbers 1 to 6 following manufacturer's instructions. (Or stencil numbers on pockets using acrylic paint and a sponge brush as an alternative.)

2. Position gray felt strip on green lining with lower edge 2¼ inches above top edge of pocket strip; pin. Edgestitch both long edges in place by machine with matching thread. Position and edgestitch eight 1×¼-inch strips spaced about 1 inch apart to make center dashed line on gray felt road.

3. Turn under 1 inch of cotton webbing on one short end to make a 1×5-inch strip. Sew across folded end to secure. Place 1-inch loop portion of Velcro over folded end and edgestitch (Diagram 2). Position raw short end of webbing strip with loop tape facedown, centering length over dashed line on felt road (Diagram 3). Baste only short raw edge to lining.

4. Using patterns on Pattern Page H, trace a car onto paper side of fusible-web square. Cut out fusible-web shape roughly ¼ inch outside traced lines. Following manufacturer's instructions, press fusible-web shape onto back of gray polka-dot scrap; let cool. Cut out car shape on drawn line; peel off paper backing.

5. With wrong sides together, fold denim rectangle in half lengthwise; then fold resulting 17×5-inch strip into thirds, folding under top and bottom edges (Diagram 4). Pin car appliqué 1 inch above bottom fold. Unfold denim and fuse car in place with a hot iron, following manufacturer's instructions. Machine-zigzag-stitch around car. Position blue felt wheels on car and edgestitch in place with a straight stitch. Center 1-inch square of hook portion of Velcro 1 inch above roof of car and edgestitch.

6. Referring to Diagram 5 and aligning raw edges, pin corded piping around perimeter of 17×10-inch denim rectangle. Baste using a scant ½-inch seam allowance and a zipper foot.

7. Layer lining and denim rectangle right sides together with car appliqué and road both at top long edge; pin. Sew pieces together using a ½-inch seam allowance and a zipper foot (sew with denim side up and stitch just inside basting stitches), leaving a 3-inch opening for turning. Turn caddy right side out; press. Machine- or hand-stitch opening closed.

8. Fold caddy in half lengthwise; press fold. Open caddy and stitch a straight line from end to end using pressed line as a guide. This will make caddy easier to fold. Fold caddy in half so road is on top of pockets. Then fold it in thirds, wrapping strap around to front so Velcro meets to complete caddy.

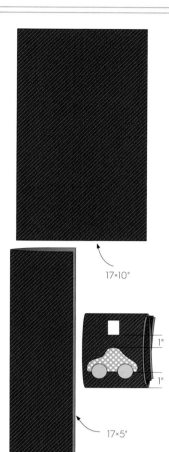

17×10"

17×5"

DIAGRAM 4

17×10"

3" | 2¾" | 2¾" | 2¾" | 2¾" | 3"

DIAGRAM 1

17×3½"

1"

DIAGRAM 2

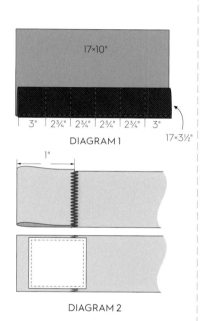

DIAGRAM 3

DIAGRAM 5

069
toss together a bean bag game

Tossing or juggling beanbags is a traditional Japanese children's game called otedama. Here's how you can stitch your own fun.

YOU WILL NEED

FOR FIVE BEAN BAGS

10—5-inch squares assorted prints

Small dried beans or rice

Finished Beanbag: approximately 2½-inch diameter

Measurements include ¼-inch seam allowances unless otherwise indicated. Sew with right sides together unless otherwise indicated.

From assorted prints, cut:
20—1¾×3½-inch strips (10 sets of 2 matching strips)

FOR CARRY BAG

¼ yard cream print

8-inch square white-and-blue dot

4×8-inch rectangle blue floral

Lightweight iron-on fusible web

1 yard ¼-inch-wide ribbon or trim

Pinking shears

Finished Carry Bag: 6×6¾×1¾ inches

Yardages and cutting instructions are based on 42 inches of usable fabric width.

CUT THE PIECES

From cream print, cut:
2—6½×9-inch rectangles

From fusible web, cut:
1—7-inch square
1—3×7-inch rectangle

From ribbon, cut:
2—18-inch-long pieces

ASSEMBLE BEANBAGS

1. For one beanbag, gather two sets of two matching print 1¾×3½-inch strips (four strips total). Mark center of long edges of each strip (A).

2. Layer two contrasting strips (B). Begin stitching at one corner, starting

and stopping ¼ inch from corner of bottom strip.

3. Pivot and sew to corner of top strip (C); pivot again and sew bottom strip to top strip's short edge, forming a "square" with three sides, to make a pieced section (D).

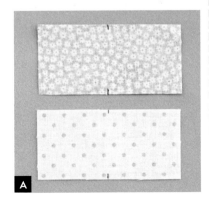

A

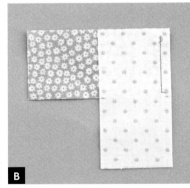

B

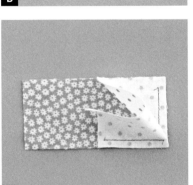

C

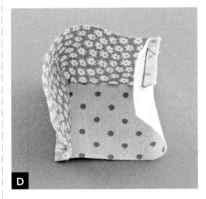

D

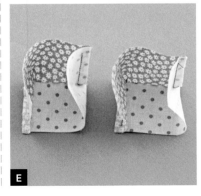

E

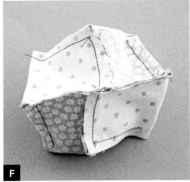

F

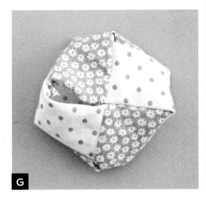

G

4. Repeat Steps 2 and 3 to make a second pieced section (E).

5. To join pieced sections, match the marked center of a rectangle on one pieced section to the unstitched corner of contrasting rectangle on the other pieced section. Sew together sections as before (F), leaving a small opening for turning.

6. Turn the right side out (G). Stuff loosely with dried beans or rice. Hand-stitch opening closed to make one beanbag.

7. Repeat Steps 1 through 6 to make five beanbags total.

ASSEMBLE CARRY BAG

1. Following manufacturer's instructions, press fusible-web 7-inch square onto wrong side of white-and-blue dot 8-inch square.
Cut fused square to make:
2—2×6½-inch strips
2—¾×6½-inch strips

2. In same manner, press fusible-web 3×7-inch rectangle to wrong side of blue floral 4×8-inch rectangle. Cut fused rectangle to make two 1×6½-inch strips.

3. Trim each white-and-blue dot ¾×6½-inch strip to ¼ inch wide, using pinking shears on one long edge only. Trim each white-and-blue dot 2×6½-inch strip to 1¾ inches wide, using pinking shears on both long edges.

4. Peel off paper backings on all strips. Following manufacturer's instructions, fuse a white-and-blue dot ¼×6½-inch strip 1¼ inches from one short edge of a cream print 6½×9-inch rectangle (Diagram 1). Fuse a blue floral 1×6½-inch strip ¼ inch above just-added strip, fuse a white-and-blue dot 1¾×6½-inch strip ¼ inch above last strip. Straight- or zigzag-stitch long edges of strips to make front. Repeat to make back.

5. Zigzag-stitch side and bottom edges of bag front and bag back.

6. Mark each side edge of bag front 3 inches from upper edge.

7. Sew together bag front and bag back along bottom and side edges, matching trims and stopping at markings (Diagram 2).

8. Turn under and topstitch a narrow hem along unstitched portion of each side edge (Diagram 3).

9. To make front ribbon casing, press top edge of bag front under ¼ inch; turn edge under again ¾ inch and press (Diagram 4). Edgestitch lower fold, backstitching at side edges. Repeat with bag back to make bag body.

10. To shape bag bottom, at one corner match bottom seam line to side seam line, creating a flattened triangle (Diagram 5). Measuring

1 inch from point of triangle, draw a 1¾-inch-long line across triangle. Sew on drawn line. Trim excess fabric, leaving ¼-inch seam allowance. Repeat with remaining corner. Turn bag body right side out.

11. Referring to Diagram 6, thread each 18-inch-long ribbon piece through the casings from opposite sides and knot ends to complete the carry bag.

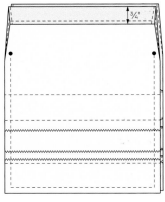

1¾×6½"

¼"

1×6½

¼"

¼×6½"

1¼"

DIAGRAM 1

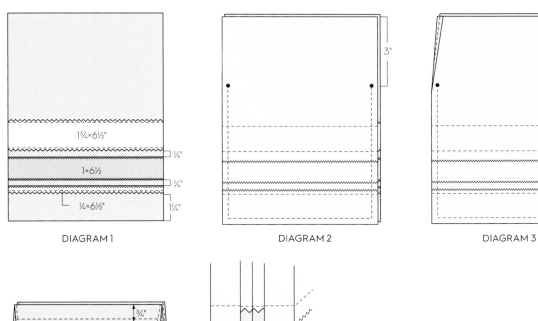

3"

DIAGRAM 2

DIAGRAM 3

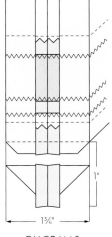

¾"

DIAGRAM 4

1"

1¾"

DIAGRAM 5

DIAGRAM 6

070

sew a sleep sack

Skip the uncomfortable ground and cold nighttime camping weather and let the kids snuggle up inside an appliqué fox sleep sack on the living room floor.

YOU WILL NEED

1 yard light blue print (top)

1⅛ yards fox novelty print (top lining, front)

½ yard multicolor arrow print (top)

1 yard rust check (appliqué, binding)

1 fat quarter (18×22-inch piece) light tan print (appliqué)

1 fat eighth (9×22-inch piece) small black dot (appliqué)

2 yards tan arrow print (back)

1¾ yards woodland polka dot (back lining)

58×60-inch piece of batting

1 yard lightweight fusible web

Sewing thread: black and cream

Finished Sleep Sack: 28×59 inches

Patterns are on Pattern Page L.

CUT THE PIECES

From light blue print, cut:
1—6×28-inch strip
1—21×28-inch rectangle

From fox novelty print, cut:
1—6×28-inch strip
1—28×44-inch rectangle

From multicolor arrow print, cut:
1—12½×28-inch strip

From rust check, cut:
6—2½×42-inch binding strips

From woodland polka dot, cut:
1—28×59-inch rectangle

From tan arrow print, cut:
1—28×52-inch rectangle
1—28×15-inch rectangle

From batting, cut:
1—28×44-inch rectangle
1—28×59-inch rectangle

ASSEMBLE TOP

1. Referring to Quilt Top Assembly Diagram, sew light blue print 6×28-inch strip and light blue print 21×28-inch rectangle to opposite edges of fox novelty print 6×28-inch rectangle. Press seams toward the fox novelty print. Add 12½×28-inch multicolor arrow print rectangle to bottom edge of unit. Press seam toward multicolor print.

2. Trace patterns on Pattern Page L onto white paper. Trace fox beard (A), head (B), eyes and nose (C), eyebrows (D, D reversed), and ears (E, E reversed) onto paper side of fusible web; leave 1 inch space between shapes. Cut around shapes.

3. With fusible side down, press shapes onto wrong sides of fabrics. Press pattern A on light tan print, Pattern B onto rust check, three of Pattern C on black dot, Pattern D and Pattern D reversed on black dot, and Pattern E and Pattern E reversed on black dot. Cut out shapes on lines.

4. Position appliqués onto light blue print 20½×28-inch rectangle ➲

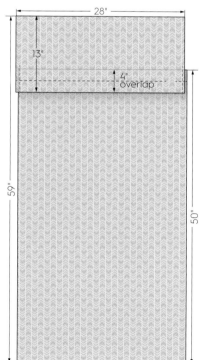

DIAGRAM 2

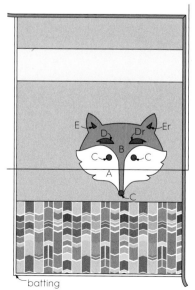

DIAGRAM 1

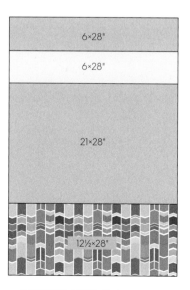

QUILT TOP ASSEMBLY DIAGRAM

⭢ (Diagram 1), placing pieces to right of center. Place tan print A piece down first. Peel off paper backings and fuse in place.

5. Machine-blanket-stitch around all appliqué edges, using black thread for all appliqués except cheeks. Use cream thread for cheeks.

6. Layer top, 28×44-inch batting rectangle, and fox novelty print 28×44-inch rectangle (Diagram 1); baste. Stitch in ditch of each seam.

7. Bind top and right sides of quilt top, leaving beginning and end of binding strip unfinished (Diagram 1). (For details, see #094.)

ASSEMBLE BACK

1. Turn under 2 inches along one 28-inch-long edge of the tan arrow 28×52-inch rectangle; press and topstitch folded edge. Repeat with 28×15-inch rectangle.

2. Overlap hemmed edges of sleep sack back pieces about 4 inches to make a 28×59-inch rectangle (Diagram 2). Stitch across overlaps on side edges to make sleep sack back.

3. Layer sleep sack back, 28×59-inch batting rectangle, and woodland polka dot 28×59-inch rectangle; baste. Measure 20 inches below top edge of back and sew seam across the width of sleep sack back through all layers to make pillow enclosure (Diagram 3).

4. With envelope-style closure facedown, use binding strips to bind top and right side edges only.

FINISH SLEEP SACK

1. Place top, appliqué side up, on top of back with envelope-style closure facedown, aligning bottom and side edges (Diagram 4). Use binding strips to bind left and bottom edges of sleep sack (Diagram 5).

2. Machine-stitch lower right side of sleep sack closed, stitching just inside the binding strips through all layers and ending 12 inches above bottom right corner (at top of multicolor arrow print strip) (Diagram 5).

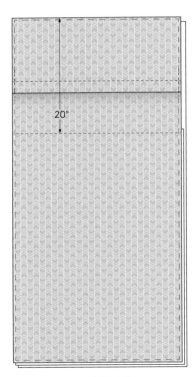

DIAGRAM 3

DIAGRAM 4

DIAGRAM 5

make the bed

Be creative on behalf of your beloved fur balls with this project handmade just for them.

YOU WILL NEED

FOR SMALL DOG BED

⅝ yard brown-and-white print (sides)
1 yard brown stripe (top and bottom)
1 yard muslin (lining)
Polyester fiberfill

FOR MEDIUM DOG BED

⅝ yard green polka dot (sides)
1¼ yards green print (top and bottom)
¾ yard green stripe (piping)
1⅞ yards muslin (lining)
5 yards of ⅜-inch-diameter cotton cording
Polyester fiberfill

FOR LARGE DOG BED

⅞ yard brown paw print (sides)
1⅝ yards brown dog print (top and bottom)
2½ yards muslin (lining)
Polyester fiberfill

Finished Dog Bed Sizes:
Small: 20×15×3 inches
Medium: 24×18×4 inches
Large: 36×27×5 inches

Yardages and cutting instructions are based on 42 inches of usable fabric width. Measurements include ½-inch seam allowances. Sew with right sides together unless otherwise stated.

ASSEMBLE SMALL DOG BED

From brown-and-white print, cut:
2—4×21-inch A rectangles
2—4×16-inch B rectangles

From brown stripe, cut:
2—16×21-inch C rectangles

From muslin, cut:
2—16×21-inch C rectangles
2—4×21-inch A rectangles
2—4×16-inch B rectangles

1. Lay a brown-and-white print A rectangle right side down on a flat surface. Aligning edges, place muslin A rectangle on top. Baste together around all sides, ¼ inch from edges. Repeat with remaining brown-and-white print and muslin A rectangles.

2. Repeat Step 1 to baste corresponding muslin rectangles to brown-and-white print and brown stripe B and C rectangles.

3. Mark each corner on muslin side of C rectangles with a dot ½ inch from edges (Diagram 1).

4. Beginning and ending seams ½ inch from edges, sew together short ends of A and B rectangles. Repeat, alternating A and B rectangles, to make a loop (Diagram

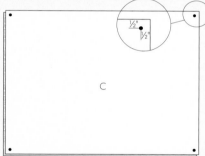

DIAGRAM 1

2, next page). Press all seams open.

5. Join one long edge of loop to a C rectangle, matching seams of loop to corner dots (Diagram 3, next page).

6. Repeat Step 6, joining remaining C rectangle to unsewn edge of loop and leaving a 6-inch opening for turning.

7. Turn right side out through opening. Stuff as desired with fiberfill. Hand-sew opening closed to complete small dog bed.

ASSEMBLE MEDIUM DOG BED

From green polka dot, cut:
2—5×25-inch A rectangles
2—5×19-inch B rectangles

From green print, cut:
2—19×25-inch C rectangles

From green stripe, cut:
Enough 2½-inch-wide bias strips to total 180 inches in length for piping

From muslin, cut:
2—19×25-inch C rectangles
2—5×25-inch A rectangles
2—5×19-inch B rectangles

1. Using pieces just cut, refer to Assemble Small Dog Bed, Steps 1 through 4.

2. Sew together green stripe 2½-inch-wide bias strips to make one long strip. Press seams open. Cover cording with strip to make piping (for details, see Make Custom Piping, right).

3. Aligning raw edges, baste piping around edges of each C rectangle. When attaching the piping to C rectangle, begin stitching 1½ inches from piping's folded end. When you reach a marked dot at a corner of the C rectangle, clip seam allowance of piping almost up to stitching. Ease piping in place along next edge, rounding corner slightly, and continue stitching. Turn each corner in same manner.

When you are 2 to 3 inches from the starting point, end stitching. Remove 1 inch of stitching at each end of the piping and pull back the bias strip ends. Cut end of cording so it fits snugly into folded opening at beginning. The ends of cording should abut inside the covering. Refold bias strip so it covers cording, lapping folded end over raw end. Finish stitching piping to C rectangle.

4. Referring to Assemble Small Dog Bed, Steps 5 through 7, join loop to C pieces, turn right side out, stuff, and sew opening closed to complete medium dog bed.

ASSEMBLE LARGE DOG BED

From brown paw print, cut:
2—6×37-inch A rectangles
2—6×28-inch B rectangles

From brown dog print, cut:
2—28×37-inch C rectangles

From muslin, cut:
2—28×37-inch C rectangles
2—6×37-inch A rectangles
2—6×28-inch B rectangles

Using pieces just cut, refer to Assemble Small Dog Bed, Steps 1 through 7 to make large dog bed.

MAKE CUSTOM PIPING

Piping is made by sewing a bias-cut fabric strip around a length of cording. The width of the bias strip will vary depending on the diameter of your cording. We used a 2½-inch-wide bias strip and ⅜-inch-diameter cording for the medium dog bed.

Fold under 1½ inches at one end of the bias strip with wrong side inside. Fold the strip in half lengthwise with wrong side inside. Insert the cording next to the folded edge, placing a cording end 1 inch from the fabric folded end. Using a zipper foot, sew through both fabric layers right next to cording to make piping (Diagram 4). Trim seam allowance to ½ inch.

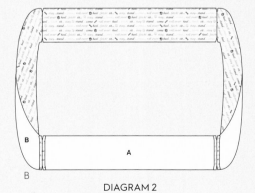

DIAGRAM 2

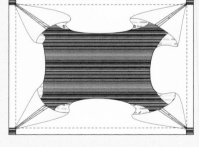

DIAGRAM 3

DIAGRAM 4

072

let the leash out

Give Fido a new leash on life with a colorful accessory to suit his personality. All you need are a purchased leash, decorative ribbon, and a few minutes of stitching.

YOU WILL NEED

Leash

Decorative ribbon, about as wide as the leash

Wash Away Wonder Tape

Embroidery thread and needle

1. Cut the ribbon to the length of the leash, allowing a ¼-inch seam allowance.

2. Use Wash Away Wonder Tape to attach the back of the ribbon to the leash and topstitch along both edges of the ribbon to secure.

Holiday Projects

Add thoughtful touches to the happy assortment under the tree with handmade projects for everyone on your list.

Special Delivery

073
trim a modern tree

Spruce up a chair or sofa for the holidays with a pretty pieced Christmas tree pillow.

YOU WILL NEED

½ yard cream-with-black-dot print fabric

⅛ yard each of light pink dot, dark pink dot, and light green dot fabric

⅛ yard of narrow red-and-white stripe fabric

¼ yard of postal print fabric

1⅛ yards of backing fabric

¼ yard of wide red-and-white stripe fabric

20-inch square of cotton batting

16-inch square pillow form

Finished Pillow: 16-inch square

Yardages and cutting instructions are based on 42 inches of usable fabric width.

Measurements include ¼-inch seam allowances unless otherwise indicated. Sew with right sides together unless otherwise indicated.

CUT THE PIECES

From cream-with-black-dot print fabric, cut:

1—3×13-inch strip

1—2½×13-inch strip

15—2⅜-inch squares, cutting each in half diagonally for a total of 30 triangles

5—1½×13-inch strips

2—1½×6¼-inch strips

2—1½×5¾-inch strips

2—1½×4¾-inch strips

2—1½×3¾-inch strips

2—1½×2¾-inch strips

2—1½×1¾-inch strips

From each light pink dot, dark pink dot, and green dot fabric, cut:

5—2⅜-inch squares, cutting each in half diagonally for a total of 10 triangles of each print

From green dot fabric, cut:

1—1½-inch square

From narrow red-and-white stripe fabric, cut:

1—1×16-inch strip

From postal print fabric, cut:

1—3½×16-inch strip

From backing fabric, cut:

1—20-inch square

2—16×20-inch rectangles

From wide red-and-white stripe fabric, cut:

2—2½×42-inch binding strips

ASSEMBLE PILLOW TOP

1. Sew together one cream-with-black-dot print triangle and one light pink dot triangle to make a triangle-square (Diagram 1). Press seam toward light pink dot triangle. The triangle square should be 1½-inch square including seam allowances. Repeat to make 10 triangle-squares total.

2. Repeat Step 1, using 10 dark pink dot triangles and 10 green dot triangles to make 20 additional triangle-squares total (Diagram 1).

3. Referring to the Tree Unit Assembly Diagram below, lay out the cream-with-black-dot print strips, the light pink dot triangle-squares, the dark pink dot triangle-squares, the green dot triangle-squares, and the green dot 1½-inch square in rows. Note the orientation of pink and green triangle-squares.

4. Sew together pieces in each row. Press seams toward squares. Join rows. Press seams in one direction. The tree unit should be 13×16 inches.

5. Fold 1×16-inch narrow red-and-white stripe strip in half lengthwise with wrong sides together. Pin the strip to left edge of tree unit (Diagram 2).

6. Sew the 3½×16-inch postal print strip to left edge of tree unit with the red-and-white strip sandwiched in between; press toward postal print to complete the pillow top.

7. Layer pillow top, 20-inch batting square, and 20-inch backing rectangle; quilt as desired, such as quilting the pillow top with vertical lines stitched ½ inch apart. Trim pillow top to 16-inch square.

FINISH PILLOW

1. With wrong sides inside, fold two 16×20-inch backing fabric rectangles in half to form two double-thick 10×16-inch rectangles. Overlap folded edges by about 4 inches to make a 16-inch square (See Pillow Back Assembly Diagram). Stitch across overlaps on side edges to make pillow back.

2. Layer pillow top and pillow back; baste. Use wide red-and-white stripe print binding strips to bind the pillow edges. (For details, see #094.)

3. Insert pillow form into pillow through envelope closure.

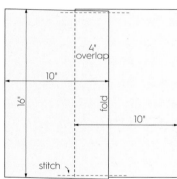

PILLOW BACK ASSEMBLY DIAGRAM

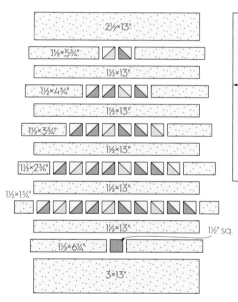

TREE UNIT ASSEMBLY DIAGRAM

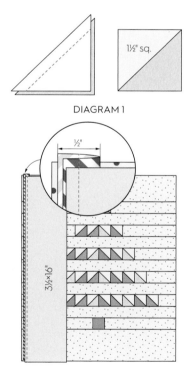

DIAGRAM 1

DIAGRAM 2

074
set a festive table

Sew a new family heirloom to use year after year.

YOU WILL NEED

¼ yard of white print fabric

18×22-inch piece (fat quarter) of red print fabric

½ yard total of holiday prints

½ yard total of assorted solid fabrics

⅝ yard of backing fabric

Fusible web

48 assorted ¼-inch- to ½-inch-diameter buttons: white

Hand-sewing needle

Sewing thread: white

23×49-inch quilt batting

Finished Size: 16½×43 inches

Yardages and cutting instructions are based on 42 inches of usable fabric width.

Measurements include ¼-inch seam allowances unless otherwise indicated. Sew with right sides together unless otherwise indicated.

CUT THE PIECES

From white print, cut:

3—2×42-inch binding strips
2—1½×16½-inch sashing strips

From red print, cut:

2—8¾×16½-inch strips

From assorted holiday prints, cut:

12—4½-inch squares

From assorted solid fabrics, cut:

12—4½-inch squares

APPLIQUÉ THE TABLE RUNNER ENDS

1. Trace the snowflake circle A, B, C, and D patterns on Pattern Page L the number of times indicated onto the paper side of fusible web, leaving ½ inch between the shapes. Cut out around the shapes. Press the shapes,

fusible side down, onto the wrong side of the white print fabric. Cut out the shapes.

2. Press fusible web, fusible side down, onto the wrong side of the remaining white print fabric.

From the web-backed fabric, cut:

6—¼×3¼-inch strips (snowflake 1)
6—¼×4¾-inch strips (snowflake 2)
6—¼×3¾-inch strips (snowflake 3)

3. Referring to the Appliqué Placement Diagram, arrange the circles from Step 1 and the strips from Step 2 to make three snowflakes on each 8¾×16½-inch red print rectangle. Remove the paper backings and press the shapes, overlapping the pieces as shown. Topstitch the pieces.

4. Referring to the photo, opposite, sew white buttons between the white print strips of each snowflake using white sewing thread.

FINISH THE TABLE RUNNER

1. Lay the 4½-inch holiday print and solid squares in four rows of six squares each, alternating the prints and solids. Sew together the pieces in each row (Diagram 1). Press seams in alternating directions. Join rows. Press seams in alternating directions.

2. Sew a 1½×16½-inch white print strip to each short side of the pieced table runner center (Diagram 2).

Press seams toward squares.

3. Sew an appliquéd table runner end to each long edge of the pieced table runner center (Runner Assembly Diagram). The completed top should measure 16½×43 inches.

4. Layer the table runner top, batting, and backing fabric rectangle; baste; quilt as desired and bind with the white print binding strips. (For details, see #093.)

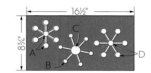

APPLIQUÉ PLACEMENT DIAGRAM

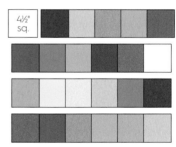

DIAGRAM 1

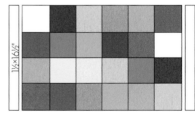

DIAGRAM 2

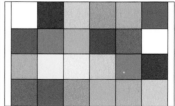
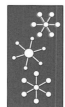

RUNNER ASSEMBLY DIAGRAM

075
whip up a holiday hot pad

Share the season with friends through a batch of homemade cookies and a matching hot pad.

YOU WILL NEED

2½×9-inch piece each of green dot print fabric and tan dot print fabric

2¼×9-inch piece of tan dot print fabric

4×5-inch-piece each of solid brown fabric and white felt

¼ yard of red-and-green dot print fabric

5×9-inch-piece of pink holiday novelty print fabric

¼ yard of lining print fabric

⅓ yard of insulated batting

9-inch square of red holiday novelty print fabric

1½×6-inch piece of red-and-white dot print fabric

2— ¼-inch-diameter buttons

Embroidery floss: brown, white

Embroidery needle

Fusible web

Finished Hot Pad: 9-inch square

Yardages and cutting instructions are based on 42 inches of usable fabric width.

Measurements include ¼-inch seam allowances unless otherwise indicated. Sew with right sides together unless otherwise indicated.

CUT THE PIECES

From green dot print, cut:
1—2½×9-inch strip

From tan dot print, cut
1—2¼×9-inch strip (pocket front)

From red-and-green dot print, cut:
1—¾×9-inch strip (pocket front)
1—1¾×15-inch strip (ruffle)
1—2×9-inch strip (pocket binding)

1—2½×42-inch strip (binding)

From lining print, cut:
2—7×9-inch rectangles (lining and pocket back)

From insulated batting, cut:
1—9-inch square
1—7×9-inch rectangle

EMBROIDER THE PIECES

1. Trace the word patterns on Pattern Page M onto white paper.

2. Using a light table or a sunny window, center and trace the words "You Are What You Eat" onto the 2½×9-inch green dot print strip. Trace the words "So Eat Something Sweet!" onto the 2¼×9-inch tan print strip, positioning the bottom of the letters 1½ inches below the strip's top edge.

3. Using a backstitch and three strands of brown embroidery floss, stitch the words on each fabric strip.

4. Trace the gingerbread boy pattern on Pattern Page M onto paper side of fusible web; cut around the shape. With the fusible side down, press the shape onto the wrong side of solid brown fabric. Peel off the paper backing and press the gingerbread boy onto the white felt. Cut around the gingerbread boy, leaving a scant ¹⁄₁₆-inch felt border. Referring to the pattern, satin stitch the eyes and straight-stitch the face and frosting lines using white embroidery floss.

ASSEMBLE THE POT HOLDER POCKET

1. Referring to the Pot Holder Pocket Assembly Diagram, sew the ¾×9-inch red-and-green dot print strip to the embroidered tan print strip along one long edge. Sew the 5×9-inch pink holiday print rectangle to the remaining long edge of the red-and-green dot print strip. Press toward the tan and pink rectangles.

2. Layer the pocket front atop 7×9-inch lining print rectangle with the 7×9-inch insulated batting rectangle between the layers; baste.

3. Quilt the 5×9-inch pink holiday novelty print rectangle as desired through all layers.

4. Fold the 1¾×15-inch red-and-green dot print strip in half lengthwise with wrong sides together (Diagram 1). Stitch a long running stitch ¼ inch from unfinished edges through both layers. Pull one thread end and gather the fabric to make a 9-inch-long ruffle. Sew the ruffle to the top of the tan print embroidered rectangle (Diagram 2).

5. Topstitch the gingerbread boy on the right half of the 5×9-inch pink holiday novelty print rectangle using brown thread (Diagram 2).

6. With wrong side inside, fold 2×9-inch red-and-green dot print strip in half lengthwise. With raw edges even, sew strip to lining side of the pocket. Bring folded edge to front and topstitch close to fold.

ASSEMBLE THE POT HOLDER BACK

1. Referring to the Pot Holder Back Assembly Diagram, sew the embroidered green dot print strip to 7×9-inch back lining rectangle.

2. Layer the pot holder back atop the 9-inch red holiday novelty print square with the 9-inch square of insulated batting between the layers; baste (Diagram 3). Quilt the pot holder back as desired.

3. Place the pot holder pocket atop the pot holder back, aligning bottom and side edges (Diagram 4). Baste sides and bottom.

4. With wrong side inside, fold 1½×6-inch red-and-white dot print in half lengthwise. Lightly press, then unfold. Fold long raw edges in to meet at center. Refold in half lengthwise, aligning folded edges; press again. Edgestitch folded edges. Matching raw ends, fold in half to make a loop; baste (Diagram 5).

5. Referring to Step 6 of Assemble the Pot Holder Pocket, bind the pot holder with the 2½×42-inch red-and-green dot binding strip. (For details, see #094.)

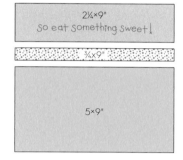

POT HOLDER POCKET ASSEMBLY DIAGRAM

DIAGRAM 1

DIAGRAM 2

POT HOLDER BACK ASSEMBLY DIAGRAM

DIAGRAM 3

DIAGRAM 4

DIAGRAM 5

076
stitch a stocking

Using one triangle template and simple quilting motifs, you can create stockings with pieced fronts or simplify with an unpieced version (center). They're perfect for containing small gifts.

YOU WILL NEED

2—18×21-inch pieces (fat quarters) contrasting prints (pieced stocking front)

18×21-inch piece (fat quarter) coordinating print (stocking back)

⅝ yard print (lining/cuff)

Lightweight fusible interfacing (such as Heat n Bond Non-Woven Fusible Featherweight interfacing)

21×30-inch lightweight cotton batting

Finished Stocking: 11¼×18⅜ inches

Yardages and cutting instructions are based on 42 inches of usable fabric width.

Measurements include ⅜-inch seam allowance unless otherwise indicated. Sew with right sides together unless otherwise indicated.

CUT THE PIECES

Patterns are on the next page.

To make a complete stocking pattern, trace Pattern B onto a large sheet of paper, extending top edge 9½ inches; enlarge and cut out.

To make a template of Pattern A, trace pattern onto template plastic. Enlarge and cut out traced shape on drawn lines. Place plastic template on wrong side of fabric and trace the number of times indicated in cutting instructions. Using a rotary cutter and ruler, cut out the pieces on drawn lines.

Note: To make a stocking with an unpieced front, do not cut 21-inch-long strips of Pattern A. Instead, cut one each of Pattern B and Pattern B reversed to make the stocking front and back. Skip Steps 1 through 3 of "Quilt and Assemble Stocking Body."

From each of two contrasting prints, cut:

6—2½×21-inch strips, using Pattern A to cut 11 triangles from each strip for 132 triangles total (66 from each print)

From scrap of one just-cut print, cut:

1—2×5-inch strip

From coordinating print, cut:

1 of Pattern B reversed

From lining/cuff print, cut:

1—10½×15½-inch rectangle
1 each of Pattern B and Pattern B reversed

From interfacing, cut:

1—10½×15½-inch rectangle

From batting, cut:

1—15×21-inch rectangle
1 of Pattern B

QUILT AND ASSEMBLE STOCKING BODY

1. Lay out contrasting print triangles in 11 rows of 12 triangles each, alternating prints (Diagram 1). Sew together triangles in each row; press seams toward darker print. Join rows to make a pieced rectangle; press seams in one direction. To save time, you can chain-piece pairs of contrasting print triangles, then join six triangle pairs for each row.

2. Place pieced rectangle right side up atop batting 15×21-inch rectangle; baste. Quilt as desired.

3. Trace Pattern B onto quilted pieced rectangle (Diagram 2). Cut out on drawn line to make stocking front.

4. Place coordinating print stocking reversed piece right side up atop stocking batting piece. Zigzag edges to make stocking back.

5. With right sides together, sew together stocking front and back with a ⅜-inch seam, leaving top edge open, to make stocking body. Turn right side out.

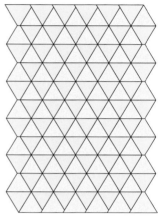

DIAGRAM 1

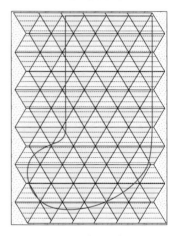

DIAGRAM 2

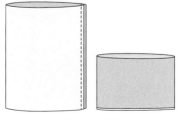

DIAGRAM 3

MAKE CUFF AND LOOP

1. Following manufacturer's instructions, fuse interfacing 10½×15½-inch rectangle to wrong side of lining/cuff print 10½×15½-inch rectangle. With right sides together, fold interfaced rectangle in half widthwise to make a 7¾×10½-inch rectangle. Sew long edges together with a ¼-inch seam allowance to make a tube (Diagram 3, previous page). Press seam in one direction. With wrong side inside, fold in half to make cuff. Topstitch folded edge if desired.

2. With wrong side inside, fold print 2×5-inch strip in half lengthwise; crease to mark center. Unfold, then fold raw edges in to meet at center. Refold strip in half along center. Topstitch along folds through all layers to make loop strip (Diagram 4).

FINISH STOCKING

1. With right sides together, sew together lining/cuff print stocking and stocking reversed pieces with a ⅜-inch seam, leaving top edge open and a 4-inch opening for turning along a straight edge, to make lining (Diagram 5). Do not turn right side out.

2. Slip cuff, folded edge down, over top of stocking body. Align raw edges; place the cuff seam at the

heel side of the stocking (Diagram 6). Fold loop strip in half and align raw edges with cuff raw edges at side seam; baste in place.

3. With right sides together, insert stocking body in lining stocking. Sew together through all layers along top raw edges with a ⅜-inch seam. Turn all layers right side out through opening in lining; hand-sew opening in lining closed. Insert lining into stocking, fold cuff down, and press flat to complete stocking.

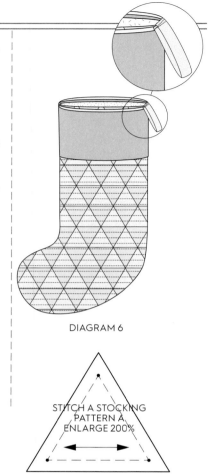

DIAGRAM 6

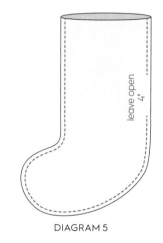

leave open 4"

DIAGRAM 5

STITCH A STOCKING
PATTERN A
ENLARGE 200%

To complete pattern, after enlarging, add 9½" above this line.

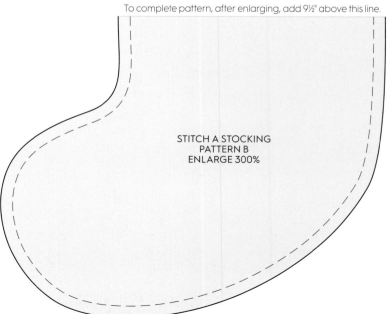

STITCH A STOCKING
PATTERN B
ENLARGE 300%

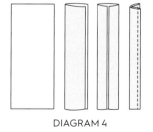

DIAGRAM 4

—Make in Minutes—

These petite mittens might not warm your hands, but they will definitely warm your heart with their charming details. Each felt mitten features blanket-stitched edges, a fabric cuff, and button details.

077
string mini mittens

YOU WILL NEED (for each mitten)

Freezer paper

9×12-inch pieces of felt: mint green, white, red, or light blue

½-inch-diameter buttons: white, mint green, red

Sewing thread: white

Needles: sewing and embroidery

Embroidery floss: white, red, light green

Polyester fiberfill

Scrap of red-and-white print

1. Lay freezer paper, shiny side down, over mitten pattern, Pattern Page M; trace two mittens for each desired mitten. Cut out freezer-paper shapes on drawn lines to make freezer-paper templates.

2. Using a hot dry iron, press each freezer-paper template, shiny side down, onto desired felt color. Lift iron to check that the template is completely (but temporarily) adhered to fabric. If template is not completely adhered, press again. Let cool. Cut out felt shapes. Carefully peel off templates.

3. Using white sewing thread, sew three buttons to the front of a felt mitten.

4. Using contrasting embroidery floss, blanket-stitch two felt mittens together, leaving the cuff end open (Diagram 1). Stuff the mitten lightly

with polyester fiberfill.

5. Cut a 1¼×4¾-inch strip from a red-and-white print. Press fabric under ¼ inch along all edges. Fold the strip in half crosswise. With the folded strip edge along the thumb side of the mitten, sandwich the open mitten cuff edge inside the folded strip; pin (Diagram 2). Topstitch the folded strip using a scant ⅛ inch along the edges.

6. Using contrasting embroidery floss, sew a button through all layers to the ends of the fabric strip; knot the floss ends, leaving 2-inch-long tails. Tie the ends of the tails together to form a hanging loop.

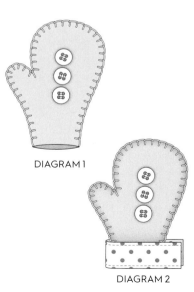

DIAGRAM 1

DIAGRAM 2

078
craft a kitchen caddy

Adorned with sweet details, such as rickrack trim and yo-yo lollipops, this gingerbread house pocket wall hanging is an irresistible place to tuck goodies, cards, or even your favorite holiday recipes. The house features three divided pockets and is adorned with a fusible-web door, easy-to-make yo-yos, rickrack trim, and buttons.

YOU WILL NEED

¼ yard of brown polka dot

¼ yard of red ticking stripe

⅜ yard of backing fabric

⅛ yard of aqua-and-white stripe

⅔ yard of ½-inch-wide rickrack: pink

Fusible interfacing

½ yard of batting

Fusible web

½ yard of ⅛-inch-wide rickrack: white

½-inch-diameter buttons: 2 pink and 1 light green

Embroidery floss: white, light green, pink

Water-soluble marking pen

Sewing thread: white

Hand-sewing needle

9—3-inch squares of assorted prints in pink, green, red, aqua, light blue

Acrylic quilter's ruler

Rotary cutter and cutting mat

10-inch length of twine

Finished Caddy: 10×10½ inches

Measurements include ¼-inch seam allowances unless otherwise indicated. Sew with right sides together unless otherwise indicated. For stitch diagrams and instructions, see #092. The patterns are on Pattern Page L.

CUT THE PIECES

From brown polka dot, cut:

1—6½×10½-inch rectangle (house body)

2—5×10½-inch rectangles (pocket front and back)

From red ticking stripe, cut:

1—5¼×10½-inch rectangle (roof)

From backing fabric, cut:

1—10½×11-inch rectangle (backing)

From aqua-and-white stripe, cut:

1—2½×10½-inch strip (binding)

From pink ½-inch-wide rickrack, cut:

2—10½-inch lengths

From fusible interfacing, cut:

1—10½×11-inch rectangle

From batting, cut:

1—10½×11-inch rectangle

1—5×10½-inch rectangle

HOW TO SEW A YO-YO

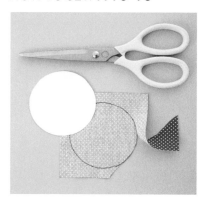

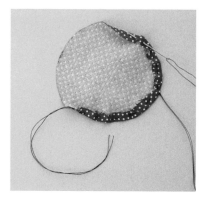

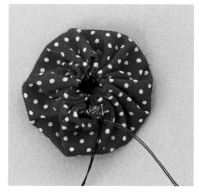

1. Trace circle pattern on Pattern Page L onto the back of an assorted print 3-inch square using a water-soluble marking pen. Cut out the circle.

2. Thread a needle with matching thread and tie a knot about 6 inches from end. With the assorted print circle facedown, turn raw edge of circle a scant ¼ inch toward circle center. Take small, evenly spaced running stitches near folded edge. End stitching next to the starting point; do not cut the thread.

3. Gently pull thread ends to gather folded edge until it forms a gathered circle. Knot thread ends to make a yo-yo; trim ends.

1. Sew pink rickrack to one long edge of brown polka-dot 6½×10½-inch rectangle. With right sides facing and along the same edge, sew red ticking stripe 5¼×10½-inch rectangle (Diagram 1). Press seam so rickrack is facing down toward house.

2. Layer interfacing on bottom, batting in middle, and house body on top with right side facing up; press.

3. To make the pocket, sandwich two brown polka-dot 5×10½-inch pieces with 5×10½-inch piece of batting in between. Sew pink rickrack to top long edge. Add binding above rickrack. (For details, see #094.)

4. Trace Door Pattern on Pattern Page L onto paper side of fusible web. Cut out around shape. Press shape onto the back of red ticking stripe 5¼×10½-inch rectangle; cut out. Peel off the paper backing and referring to Pocket Placement Diagram, center the door onto the front of the pocket, aligning the bottom of the door with the bottom edge; press. Sew white ⅛-inch-wide rickrack along the edges of the door; trim edges even with raw edges of pocket.

5. Cut two 2-inch-long and two 1¾-inch-long pieces from white ⅛-inch-wide rickrack. Referring to Pocket Placement Diagram, sew a 2-inch-long rickrack piece ¾ inch from each side of the door. Sew two 1¾-inch lengths 2¼ inches from each side of the door. Sew light green button to the door with matching embroidery floss.

6. With right sides faceup, place pocket atop house body, aligning bottom edges. Baste sides and bottom.

7. Measure 2½ inches from center of pocket and mark a vertical line with a water-soluble marking pen for a pocket divider. Repeat on opposite side. Sew each line with white sewing thread. Using pink embroidery floss, sew a button to top of each sewn line (Diagram 2).

8. Find center of red ticking stripe roof and use an acrylic quilter's ruler to mark a diagonal line from the top center point to the bottom roof corners. Trim along the lines. Fold twine in half and place folded twine at the roof point with raw edges aligned (Diagram 2).

9. Sew house body and backing fabric with right sides together, leaving a 2½-inch opening along one side and catching twine ends in seam. Trim excess backing fabric along roof peak. Turn right side out; trim the corners and press. Hand-stitch the opening closed. Embroider a running stitch using white embroidery floss along the roof, just above the rickrack.

10. Refer to the instructions on previous page to make a yo-yo. Repeat the steps to make nine yo-yos total using assorted prints.

11. Referring to photo on previous page for placement, hand-stitch five yo-yos to roof and a yo-yo to the top of each rickrack length on the pocket.

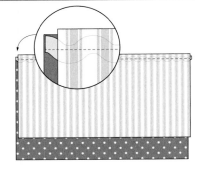

DIAGRAM 1

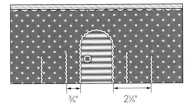

POCKET PLACEMENT DIAGRAM

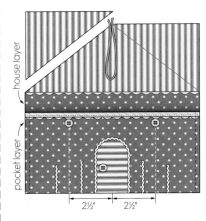

DIAGRAM 2

079
make a penguin gift bag

Bundled in cold-weather accessories, these fun-loving penguins come bearing gifts. Stiff felt allows each penguin to stand on its own and creates a three-dimensional bag body that has space inside for a small gift. Choose from two color options, then use twill ribbons for the earmuff band.

YOU WILL NEED (for one penguin)

2—9×12-inch pieces stiff wool felt: gray or black (penguin body, sides, base, wings, tail)

5×8-inch piece white wool felt (penguin belly)

6×6-inch piece of orange wool felt (penguin feet and beak)

4×12-inch piece wool felt: bright blue or chartreuse (scarf)

Worsted-weight yarn: red or bright blue

Fabric chalk marker

Air-soluble fabric marking pen

Polyester fiberfill

2—¼-inch-diameter buttons: black

2—10-inch pieces of ⅜-inch-wide twill tape: black

Short appliqué pins with small heads or fabric glue (optional)

1⅜-inch pom-pom maker

FOR GRAY PENGUIN

Scraps of felt: aqua, light blue, chartreuse

10-inch piece of ⅜-inch-wide ribbon: red-and-white polka dot

Embroidery floss: white, orange, black, red, aqua, gray, light blue, chartreuse, bright blue

FOR BLACK PENGUIN

Scraps of felt: chartreuse, bright blue, red

Embroidery floss: white, orange, black, red, aqua, black, bright blue, red, chartreuse

Finished Bags: gray penguin holding gift, 5×7½ inches plus handles; black penguin with outstretched wings, 7½×7½ inches plus handles

The patterns are on Pattern Page I.

FOR GRAY PENGUIN

From stiff gray wool felt, cut:

2 of Pattern A (front and back)

2 of Pattern B (sides)

1 of Pattern C (base)

2 of Pattern D (wing 1)

2 of Pattern F (wing 2 for black penguin)

1 of Pattern E (tail)

From white wool felt, cut:

2 of Pattern G (belly)

From orange wool felt, cut:

8 of Pattern H (foot)

2 of Pattern I (beak)

From bright blue wool felt, cut:

1—1×5-inch strip (scarf back)

2—1×10-inch strips (scarf front and sides)

From aqua wool felt, cut:

1 of Pattern L (box)

1 of Pattern M (lid)

FOR BLACK PENGUIN

From stiff black wool felt, cut:

2 of Pattern A (front and back)

2 of Pattern B (sides)

1 of Pattern C (base)

2 of Pattern F (wing 2)

1 of Pattern E (tail)

From white wool felt, cut:

2 of Pattern G (belly)

From orange wool felt, cut:

8 of Pattern H (foot)

2 of Pattern I (beak)

From chartreuse wool felt, cut:

1—1×5-inch strip (scarf back)

2—1×10-inch strips (scarf front and sides)

MAKE GRAY PENGUIN BODY FRONT

1. Use two strands of matching embroidery thread and short running stitches for all stitching unless otherwise noted for all penguins. For stitch diagrams, see #092. Stitch ⅛ inch from edges.

2. Referring to Front Appliqué Placement Diagram, lay a white belly piece atop a gray body piece; pin or glue. Stitch the belly piece to the body front piece.

3. Pin the beak to the body and stitch along two side beak edges. Lightly stuff the beak through the top opening with polyester fiberfill; then stitch along the top beak edge.

4. Stitch two black buttons to the body for eyes.

5. Cut a 1½-inch piece from red polka-dot ribbon. Referring to the photo, previous page, for ribbon placement, stitch the ribbon to the aqua box. Cut a ½-inch piece of ribbon and stitch it to the aqua lid. Cut a 3½-inch ribbon piece and overlap the ends to make a loop; stitch through the center of the loop. Cut a 1-inch length of ribbon and wrap it around the center of the loop; stitch through the center. Stitch the ribbon to the top of the lid for a bow. Stitch the box and lid to the center of the penguin belly so the bottom of the box is 1¼ inches from the bottom edge of the belly.

6. Pin two gray wing 1 pieces to the body front so they overlap the gift. Stitch in place.

MAKE GRAY PENGUIN SIDES AND BODY BACK

1. Place the gray tail on the bottom of the gray body back piece. Referring to Back Appliqué Placement Diagram, stitch the tail in place along straight edges, stopping ¼ inch from the bottom of body back.

2. Cut light blue, aqua, and chartreuse felt into ⅛×1-inch strips (you will need about 27 strips total). Lay the strips crosswise on the bright blue scarf pieces, arranging them so they are evenly spaced and leaving 2 inches uncovered on each strip end for fringe. Stitch the strips to the scarf pieces. Cut 1½-inch-long fringe on each scarf end.

3. Referring to Back Appliqué Placement Diagram, stitch scarf back to body back 2¾ inches below the top of the body back; trim scarf ends flush with side of body back.

4. Referring to Side Appliqué Placement Diagram, stitch bright blue

FRONT APPLIQUÉ PLACEMENT DIAGRAM

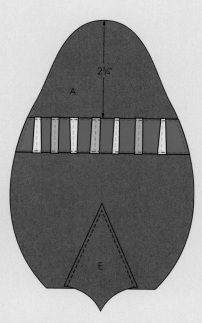

BACK APPLIQUÉ PLACEMENT DIAGRAM

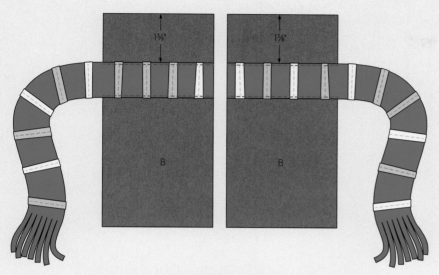

SIDE APPLIQUÉ PLACEMENT DIAGRAM

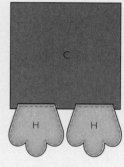

DIAGRAM 2

10-inch scarf strips to gray body side pieces, positioning the top edge of each scarf piece 1⅜ inches from the top. Trim one end of each scarf piece flush with edges of body side pieces as shown. Leave opposite end of each scarf piece long.

5. Place two orange foot pieces together, matching raw edges. Referring to the pattern, stitch the pieces together, leaving an opening where indicated. Stuff fiberfill through the opening, then stitch closed ¼ inch from the edge. Repeat to make a second foot. Referring to Diagram 2, stitch feet to base.

ASSEMBLE THE GIFT BAG

1. With wrong sides together and feet extending forward, stitch bottom of body front to front edge of the base.

2. Referring to the photo on previous page for handle placement, pin twill tape ends to back side edges of

penguin head. With wrong sides together, stitch side edges of body front to long edges of side pieces with scarf pieces extending toward front and keeping them free of stitching. Continue stitching around top of head and through twill tape ends.

3. Repeat Steps 1 and 2 to stitch the body back to the base and sides and to add a handle. Lift the tail as you stitch so you do not stitch through it.

4. Stitch bottom edge of each side piece to the side edge of the base.

5. Following the pom-pom maker manufacturer's instructions, make two 1½-inch-diameter pom-poms using red yarn. Hand-stitch each pom-pom to the head near the twill tape handle ends.

6. Tie the scarf ends together as desired. Tack in place as needed with matching embroidery floss.

MAKE BLACK PENGUIN

1. Follow Steps 1 through 3 of Make Gray Penguin Body Front, substituting black pieces for the gray pieces.

2. Place two gray wing 1 pieces together, matching raw edges. Referring to the pattern, stitch the pieces together, leaving an opening where indicated. Stuff fiberfill through the opening; then stitch the opening closed ¼ inch from the edge. Repeat with remaining wing pieces. Stitch a wing to the back of the body front at each side.

3. Follow Steps 1 through 5 of Make Gray Penguin Sides and Body Back, substituting chartreuse scarf pieces.

4. Follow Steps 1 through 6 of Assemble the Gift Bag, substituting bright blue yarn for red felt for the stripes. Substitute bright blue yarn for the pom-poms.

080
sew a snack mat for santa

Lay out an adorable snack mat just for Santa. Fusible-web appliqués of a cookie plate and a milk glass labeled with embroidered words mark the placement for Santa's Christmas Eve must-haves.

YOU WILL NEED

8-inch square of brown polka dot fabric

4-inch square of light blue polka dot fabric

⅓ yard of red-and-pink stripe fabric

Fusible web

10¾ inch-length of 1-inch-wide lace trim

10¾×8½-inch piece of batting

Hand-sewing needle and thread

Transfer paper

Old ballpoint pen or stylus

Embroidery floss: ecru, light blue, brown

Finished Mat: 10¼×8 inches

Measurements include ¼-inch seam allowances unless otherwise indicated. Sew with right sides together unless otherwise stated. Patterns are on Pattern Page M. For embroidery details, see #092.

1. Trace cookies pattern onto paper side of fusible web-backed brown polka dot; enlarge and cut out. Trace milk pattern onto paper side of fusible web-backed light blue polka dot; enlarge and cut out. With the fusible side down, press fusible web onto back side of each polka-dot print.

2. Cut 2—10¾×8½-inch rectangles from the red-and-pink stripe fabric.

3. Referring to Appliqué Placement Diagram, arrange cookie plate and milk glass appliqué shapes on one red-and-pink stripe rectangle. Remove paper backings and press the shapes.

4. With right sides together and raw edges aligned, place lace trim along one long edge of the remaining 10¾×8½-inch red-and-pink stripe rectangle from Step 2. Fold the trim ends under ¼ inch and pin lace in place (Diagram 1).

5. With right sides together, layer red-and-pink stripe 10¾×8½-inch rectangles. Place batting on top. Sew pieces together, leaving a 3-inch opening along one side. Turn right side out; slip-stitch opening closed.

6. Topstitch the cookie plate and the milk glass. Stop stitching in the exact spot where you began topstitching and pull the thread tails to the back of the mat. Tie the tails in a big knot then thread the tails onto a sewing needle. Insert the needle into the mat and pull the knot into the mat, burying the knot and thread tails in the batting.

7. To transfer designs and words to be embroidered, place the mat on a hard surface and place transfer paper on desired area with the transfer side down. Place pattern on top of the transfer paper. Using an old ballpoint pen or stylus, trace the pattern to transfer the design to be embroidered to the fabric.

8. Using a running stitch and ecru embroidery floss, stitch the circle on the cookie plate appliqué. Backstitch the word "cookies" inside the circle and stitch a small cross-stitch for the dot on the letter i.

9. Using a running stitch and light blue embroidery floss, stitch the circle on the milk glass appliqué. Backstitch the word "milk" inside the circle.

10. Backstitch the word "crumbs" on the lower right-hand corner of the mat with brown embroidery floss. Add two small cross-stitches for crumbs.

11. Stitch a running stitch line approximately ⅜ inch from the lace edge of the mat. Bury the knot at the end of the stitching as in Step 6.

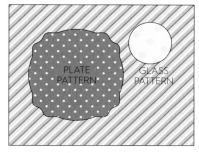

APPLIQUÉ PLACEMENT DIAGRAM

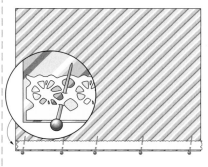

DIAGRAM 1

081
embellish with color and cheer

Wool felt is versatile, flexible, and perfect for creating this assortment of no-sewing-required holiday ornaments. The five options require minimal materials and make great decorations for hanging or tying onto packages.

YOU WILL NEED

FOR ALL ORNAMENTS
Fabric glue or quick-setting glue
String or bakers twine

FOR EACH ROSETTE ORNAMENT
Scraps of wool felt: two or three colors
Pinking shears

FOR EACH TEARDROP ORNAMENT
Scraps of wool felt: three colors
Pinking shears

FOR THE 3-D ORNAMENT
Freezer paper
9×12-inch piece each of wool felt: two colors
Two ¼-inch-diameter beads: clear

FOR THE SNOWFLAKE ORNAMENT
Freezer paper
Scraps of wool felt: two colors
Pinking shears

FOR THE POINSETTIA ORNAMENT
For small or large poinsettias:
Tracing paper and pencil
Freezer paper
Wool felt in dark red, red and white
Fabric glue
Clip clothespins
Hole punch
Ribbon or string

ROSETTE ORNAMENT (A)

1. Cut four 1×9-inch strips from desired color of wool felt.

2. Overlap ends of each strip slightly to form a circle; glue. Let dry.

3. Press down on each wool circle to create a flattened loop with the overlapped ends on the back. Place a dot of glue in the center of inside of each loop. Let dry. Layer the flattened loops to create an eight-spoke rosette with glued areas in the center. Glue the loops together at the center.

4. For the layered flower center version shown in green, opposite, trace Patterns 1A and 2A on Pattern Page O onto white paper; cut out. Use pinking shears to cut out the Pattern 1A circle from desired felt. Glue pinked-edge circle to center of rosette. Cut Pattern 2A flower from desired felt. Glue flower to center of pinked-edge circle. Let dry. For the layered flower center version shown in teal, left, trace Patterns 1B and 2B on Pattern Page O onto white paper; cut out five of 1B and one of 2B from desired felt. Glue five 1B pieces to center of rosette. Glue Pattern 2B on top.

5. Create two coiled circles with decorative yarn, ribbon, or cord. Glue a coiled circle center to each side of the ornament. Let dry.

TEARDROP ORNAMENT (B)

1. Using pinking shears, cut a ½×5-inch strip from one color of felt, a ½×6-inch from second color of felt, and a ½×8½-inch strip from third color of felt.

2. Slightly overlap ends of ½×5-inch felt strip to form a circle; glue. Let dry.

3. Repeat Step 2 with ½×6-inch strip. Place the small circle inside the large circle and glue circles together at the overlapped ends. Let dry.

4. Glue the ends of the ½×8½-inch strip together to form a teardrop shape. Let dry. Glue the felt circles inside the teardrop, aligning the overlapped ends with the glued ends of the teardrop and pinching the circles slightly into teardrop shapes.

3-D ORNAMENT (C)

1. See pattern on Pattern Page O; choose Pattern A (large) or Pattern B (small). To use freezer paper for cutting shapes, lay freezer paper, shiny side down, over pattern. Use a pencil to trace pattern 12 times onto freezer paper, leaving ¼ inch between tracings. Cut out freezer paper shapes roughly ⅛ inch outside traced lines.

2. Using a hot dry iron, press freezer paper shapes, shiny sides down, onto desired color of wool felt. Cut out shapes on lines and peel off freezer paper.

3. Cut a ½×5-inch piece of wool felt. Roll the felt into a ¼×5-inch cylinder. Glue the overlapped edges. Let dry. Trim ½ inch from the length of the cylinder.

4. Run a line of quick-setting glue along the straight edge of a felt shape and press glued edge onto cylinder. Let dry. Repeat with all remaining shapes, alternating colors as you work your way around the cylinder.

5. Cut a 7-inch length of string and thread it through one of the clear beads; knot the ends. Glue the bead to the top of the ornament. Let dry. Glue remaining clear bead to the bottom of the ornament.

SNOWFLAKE ORNAMENT (D)

1. See pattern on Pattern Page O. To use freezer paper for cutting shapes, lay freezer paper, shiny side down, over Circle Pattern. Use a pencil to trace the pattern two times onto freezer paper, leaving ¼ inch between patterns. Cut out freezer paper shapes roughly ⅛ inch outside traced lines.

2. Using a hot dry iron, press freezer paper circles, shiny sides down, onto colors of felt. Cut on lines.

3. Fold one circle in half. Take small cuts along fold and along curved edge. Open circle and refold in opposite direction. Make a second set of cuts along fold and curved edge; unfold. Repeat to make a third and fourth set of cuts.

4. Glue snowflake to circle. Cut a 7-inch length of bakers twine and glue the ends to the top back of the circle for a hanging loop. Let dry.

POINSETTIA ORNAMENT (E)

1. See pattern on Pattern Page O. Trace pattern onto tracing paper; cut out.

2. Using an iron on medium heat, press freezer paper, shiny side down, onto felt. Place patterns on the freezer paper; trace Large or Small Poinsettia on dark red felt and five Large or Small Leaves on red felt. Cut out shapes and peel off freezer paper.

3. Dab fabric glue on right side of one corner of each leaf; pinch together, holding in place with a clothespin. Repeat for each leaf. Let dry; remove clothespins. Apply fabric glue to back of leaf; glue to poinsettia between petals. Repeat with other leaves. Use a hole punch to create five dots from white felt for red flower and five dots from red felt for white flower. Glue a dot over glued seam of each folded petal.

4. Form a loop of ribbon or string to hang ornaments from tree.

082
appliqué a doll

Russian nesting dolls, called matryoshkas, come in all different types of personalities, but perhaps the most beloved is the motherly peasant figure. Our ornament is fashioned in a traditional likeness from felt appliqué.

WHAT YOU NEED

Water-soluble marking pen

8×9-inch piece of wool or wool-blend felt: turquoise

5×6-inch piece of wool or wool-blend felt: white

Scraps of wool or wool-blend felt: yellow, pink, red, green

Embroidery hoop and needle

Embroidery floss: black and colors to match felt

Fabric glue

Polyester fiberfill

PREPARE THE PATTERN

1. Trace patterns on Pattern Page P onto white paper and cut out. Using a water-soluble marking pen, trace outlines for two bodies on turquoise felt, one face and one apron on white, one hair shape on yellow, two cheeks on pink, five petals on red, and two leaves on green. Cut out hair, cheeks, petals, and leaves.

EMBROIDER THE FRONT

1. Use two strands of floss for all embroidery. Using marking pen, draw eyes and mouth on face and backstitch using black floss. Glue cheeks and hair to face and flower petals and leaves to apron. Referring to photo and using split stitches and green floss, outline leaves, make leaf veins, and work two side-by-side rows of split stitches for a stem. Outline just inside cheeks with pink running stitches and just inside flower petals with red running stitches. Add pink French knots between petals and for flower center.

2. Cut out face and apron and glue to body front. Referring to photo, outline hair with yellow split stitches and lower portion of face and all around apron with white split stitches. Outline face and apron again, using turquoise split stitches and placing stitches on turquoise felt. Cut out body front and back.

FINISH THE ORNAMENT

1. Cut a 10-inch length of turquoise floss and fold it in half to form a hanging loop. Glue ends to wrong side of body back at top of head. Let glue dry. With wrong sides together and using turquoise floss and blanket stitches, sew together body pieces, stuffing shape with fiberfill as you stitch.

—Make in Minutes—

Give the wine-lover on your list a set of embroidered felt coasters that are not only fun and colorful but also a clever way for party guests to identify their glasses.

083
sip in style

YOU WILL NEED

Felt in desired colors

Water-soluble marking pen

13 inches of contrasting pom-pom trim

Fabric glue*

Embroidery floss to match pom-pom trim

1. Trace circle on Pattern Page S onto white paper and trace the dashed lines onto the center; cut out the circle and cut along the dashed lines, cutting out the gray square indicated in the center of the pattern.

2. Using the pattern, cut two circles from felt. Using a water-soluble marking pen, trace the square opening and draw along the cut lines onto the center of one circle; cut along the drawn lines and remove the felt square from the center.

3. Using fabric glue, adhere the pom-pom trim to the outside edge of the felt circle without the center opening, overlapping ends. Let dry.

4. Using six strands of embroidery floss, stitch French knots, running stitches, cross stitches, or straight stitches about ¼ inch inside the outside edge of the felt circle with the center opening.

5. With the wrong side facing up, run a thin line of fabric glue around the edge of the felt circle with the pom-pom trim. Place embroidered felt circle on top. Let dry.

*__Note:__ Fabric glue can save a lot of time over hand stitching. Apply it sparingly and allow to dry fully before using the piece. Most fabric glues are even machine washable.

084
take stock of the season

Vibrant colors and shapes make these no-sewing-needed stockings instant heirlooms.

YOU WILL NEED (for each stocking)
Freezer paper
18×24-inch rectangle of wool felt
Scraps of wool felt
Quick-setting gel glue
¾×46-inch strip of wool felt
Pinking shears

FOR SNOWFLAKE STOCKING

1. Trace stocking pattern on Pattern Page P onto white paper.

Cut freezer paper into 5×7-inch sheets; flatten sheets under a stack of books. Trace desired snowflake patterns onto dull sides of freezer-paper sheets. Separate the snowflakes.

2. Using the stocking pattern, cut a stocking front and a stocking back from white felt. Using a dry iron on medium heat, press freezer-paper snowflakes, shiny sides down, on desired colors of felt scraps. Cut out shapes and carefully peel off freezer paper.

3. Referring to the photo, opposite, arrange snowflakes on stocking front; adhere with quick-setting gel glue. Trim away excess parts of snowflakes. Glue the ¾×46-inch turquoise blue strip to wrong side of stocking front, starting and stopping at the top edge and letting strip extend about ⅜ inch beyond stocking edges as trim. Glue the stocking back to the stocking front, leaving open at the top.

4. Cut along the turquoise blue trim with pinking shears. From remaining white felt, cut a 1×10-inch strip for a hanging loop. Fold strip in half crosswise and glue ends inside stocking to stocking back, referring to photo for placement.

FOR CIRCLES STOCKING

1. Trace stocking pattern on Pattern Page P onto white paper. Cut a stocking front and a stocking back from white felt.

Prepare the circle and star patterns on Pattern Page Q and cut the felt following instructions for Snowflake Stocking.
Note: Cut out some circles using pinking shears.

2. Referring to the photo, opposite, glue circles and starbursts to stocking front with quick-setting gel glue. Assemble and finish stocking as directed for Snowflake Stocking.

FOR STRIPES STOCKING

1. Trace stocking pattern with heel and toe on Pattern Page P onto white paper; set aside. Trace the snowflake pattern on Pattern Page Q onto white paper, following instructions for the Snowflake Stocking. **Note:** Trace two desired snowflakes onto dull sides of freezer-paper sheets.

2. Using the patterns, cut a stocking front and a stocking back from turquoise blue felt and a heel and toe from lime felt.

Referring to photo, cut felt scraps into various-size strips to fit stocking front, trimming some with pinking shears. From brown felt, cut two ⅜×8-inch strips to outline inside edges of heel and toe. Using a dry iron on medium heat, press the freezer-paper snowflake shapes, shiny sides down, on light blue and turquoise blue felt. Cut out shapes

and carefully peel off freezer paper. Cut light blue snowflake in half.

3. Referring to photo, arrange various-size strips on stocking front and adhere with quick-setting gel glue. Glue turquoise blue snowflake and light blue snowflake halves on a wide white strip. Glue heel and toe shapes on stocking front. Adhere the ⅜×8-inch brown strips to inside edges of heel and toe and trim excess felt.

Assemble and finish stocking as directed for Snowflake Stocking, using a ¾×46-inch white strip as trim and adding a turquoise blue hanging loop.

Special Delivery

085
make a special delivery gift tag

Here's proof that handmade tags can be as special as the gift itself.

YOU WILL NEED

9×12-inch piece of fusible web

6-inch square of floral print

6-inch square of taupe linen

9×12-inch piece of white felt

Hand-sewing needle and thread

3×5-inch piece of cream solid

Water-soluble marking pen

Embroidery floss: brown

Embroidery needle

3×5-inch piece of brown print

4-inch length of twill ribbon:
cream-and-red stripe

Fabric glue

4-inch square of green-and-white stripe

2—¼-inch-diameter grommets: silver

12-inch length of bakers twine:
silver-and-white

1. With fusible side down, press fusible web onto back side of floral print. Trace Tag B pattern on Pattern Page L onto paper side of fusible web; cut out.

2. With fusible side down, press a separate piece of fusible web onto back of taupe linen. Remove paper; place linen on white felt; press.

3. Remove paper from floral print tag shape and place the shape on taupe linen; press. Carefully cut around tag shape, leaving about ⅛ inch of linen showing around the tag shape. Topstitch tag shape to tag front using matching sewing thread.

4. Using a water-soluble marking pen, trace pattern onto cream solid fabric. With fusible side down, press a separate piece of fusible web onto back side of the cream fabric. Remove paper and press cream fabric onto white felt. Cut out shape on lines. Using two strands of embroidery floss and an embroidery needle, backstitch the words "Special Delivery" on Pattern Page N.

5. With fusible side down, press fusible web onto the back side of the felt-backed embroidered rectangle. Remove paper and press the rectangle onto brown print. Carefully cut around rectangle, leaving about ¹⁄₁₆ inch of brown print showing around the rectangle.

6. Cut a V-shape notch at each end of twill ribbon. Adhere the ribbon to center of tag using fabric glue. Let dry.

7. Center the cream embroidered rectangle on the tag front with the ribbon running through the center. Topstitch around cream rectangle.

8. Trace the bird (Pattern Page N) onto the paper side of the fusible

web; cut out. With fusible side down, press fusible web onto the back side of the green-and-white stripe fabric. Press green-and-white stripe bird onto white felt. Cut around bird, leaving ⅛ inch of white felt showing.

9. Following manufacturer's instructions, insert a grommet through the top of the tag and through one of the bird's wings. Tie twine through the grommet at the top of the tag for a hanger. Thread the twine tails through the grommet in the bird's wing and tie to secure.

086
put a poinsettia on it

This pretty poinsettia will stay fresh all year long.

YOU WILL NEED

6-inch square of taupe linen

4×6-inch piece of fusible interfacing

4×6-inch piece of fusible web

5-inch square each of three pink prints

9×12-inch piece of white felt

Sewing thread: white

Hand-sewing needle

3-mm seed beads: pink

¼-inch-diameter silver grommet

12-inch-length of bakers twine:
white-and-gold

1. Trace Tag A patterns on Pattern Page L onto white paper; cut out. Cut the following pieces:

From taupe linen, cut:
2 of Tag A (tag front and tag back)

From fusible interfacing cut:
1 of Tag A

2. Following manufacturer's instructions and aligning raw edges, fuse interfacing to wrong side of linen tag front. With right sides together, sew tag front and tag back, leaving a 2-inch opening along one side. Turn right side out and hand-stitch the opening closed. Topstitch around the tag 's edges.

3. Trace small, medium, and large poinsettias (Pattern Page N) onto the paper side of fusible web, leaving 1 inch between shapes; cut out.

4. With the fusible side down, press one fusible-web shape onto the back side of one print. Repeat with remaining shapes and remaining prints. Cut out shapes on the lines.

5. Remove paper from fusible-web shapes and place the shapes on the white felt; press shapes. Carefully cut around each print, leaving 3 mm of white felt showing around each print.

6. Starting at the center of a flower, topstitch using white sewing thread through center of each petal to the tip, then back to center. Topstitch each poinsettia in this manner.

7. Layer poinsettias with the largest on the bottom and the smallest on top, offsetting the petals as shown in the photo, previous page. Hand-stitch through the center of the stack, then stitch the stack to the front of the tag, offsetting it slightly to the right of center. Sew seed beads to the center of stack.

8. Following manufacturer's instructions, insert a grommet through top of the tag. Tie bakers twine through grommet for a hanger.

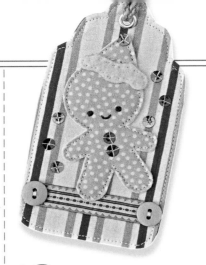

087
tag it with a treat

This whimsical tag is almost as sweet as the real stuff.

YOU WILL NEED

- **6-inch square of pink-and-cream stripe**
- **4×6-inch piece of fusible interfacing**
- **9×12-inch piece of white felt**
- **3-inch square of tan print**
- **Scrap of green print**
- **2⅛-inch-length of ribbon: red-and-green**
- **Fabric glue**
- **Sewing thread: white**
- **Needles: hand-sewing and embroidery**
- **Water-soluble marking pen**
- **Embroidery floss: brown**
- **9 sequins: 3 blue, 2 light pink, 4 dark pink**
- **2—⁷⁄₁₆-inch-diameter buttons: pink**
- **¼-inch-diameter grommet: silver**
- **12-inch-length of bakers twine: green-and-tan**

1. Trace the Tag B patterns on Pattern Page L onto white paper; cut out. Cut the following pieces.:

From pink-and-cream stripe, cut:
2 of Tag B

From fusible interfacing, cut:
1 of Tag B

From white felt, cut:
1 of Hat Brim (Pattern Page N)

From scrap of green print, cut:
1 of Hat Crown (Pattern Page N)

2. Following manufacturer's instructions and aligning raw edges, fuse interfacing to wrong side of pink-and-cream stripe tag front.

3. With the fusible side down, press onto the back side of the tan print and green print fabrics. Remove paper from tan and green prints and place the pieces on white felt; press.

4. Trace the gingerbread boy (Pattern Page N) onto the felt-backed tan print; cut out. Trace the hat pattern onto the felt-backed green print; cut out.

5. Use fabric glue to attach the gingerbread boy, hat crown, and ribbon to the tag front. Let the glue dry. Topstitch around the tan print gingerbread boy and the green print hat crown using white thread.

6. Using a running stitch and white sewing thread, hand-stitch the hat brim to the bottom of the hat crown and the top of the gingerbread boy's head.

7. Using a water-soluble marking pen and referring to pattern, draw the gingerbread boy's face. Embroider the face with three strands of brown embroidery floss. Stitch a French knot for each eye and use backstitches for the smile.

8. Stitch two dark pink sequins to front of the gingerbread boy for buttons. Stitch one light blue sequin to the tip of hat. Stitch remaining sequins to each side of gingerbread boy on the tag front, three to a side. **Note:** To secure sequins, make stitches through center of a sequin and over the front to resemble the spokes of a wagon wheel.

9. With right sides together, sew tag front and tag back, leaving a 2-inch opening along one side. Trim the curves; press. Turn right side out and hand-stitch the opening closed. Topstitch around the edges of tag. Sew a button to each end of ribbon.

10. Following manufacturer's instructions, insert a grommet through the top of the tag. Tie bakers twine through the grommet hole for a hanger.

088
dress a package with a reindeer

The polka-dot reindeer on this gift tag wears a gold jingle bell.

YOU WILL NEED
4×6-inch piece of green-and-white pinstripe
7-inch square of fusible web
3×5-inch piece of brown print
4×6-inch piece of white felt
Sewing thread: white
Sewing needle
Scallop-edge scissors
Gold metallic thread
½-inch jingle bell
¼-inch-diameter grommet: silver
12-inch length of bakers twine

1. Trace the Tag A pattern on Pattern Page L onto white paper; cut out. Cut 1 of Tag A from green-and-white pinstripe.

2. Trace reindeer (Pattern Page N) onto paper side of fusible web; cut out. With fusible side down, press onto back side of brown print. Cut out.

3. Remove paper from fusible-web reindeer. Place the reindeer on the green-and-white pinstripe tag; press.

4. With remaining fusible web, press fusible web, paper side up, onto back of tag. Remove paper from

fusible-web tag and place tag on white felt; press. Topstitch around the green-and-white pinstripe tag shape using white sewing thread.

5. Trim the felt around using scallop-edge scissors.

6. Thread a jingle bell onto a length of metallic thread. Sew one long stitch across the reindeer's neck for a collar with the bell. Knot the thread on the back of the tag.

7. Following manufacturer's instructions, attach a grommet to the top of the tag. Thread bakers twine through the grommet for a hanger.

089
trim a gift with a tree

The simplest symbol of the season shines on this gift tag.

YOU WILL NEED
6-inch square of pink-and-white stripe
4×6-inch piece of fusible interfacing
4×6-inch piece of fusible web
3×5-inch piece of green print
3×5-inch piece of white felt
Sewing thread: white
Hand-sewing needle
2-inch length of printed word ribbon
Sequins: 5 round dark pink, 4 round light pink, 3 round silver, 1 gold star
¼-inch-diameter grommet: silver
12-inch length of bakers twine

Measurements for all tags include ¼-inch seam allowances. Sew with right sides together unless otherwise stated.

1. Trace the Tag B pattern on Pattern Page L onto white paper; cut out. Cut the following pieces:

From pink-and-white stripe, cut:
2 of Tag B

From fusible interfacing cut:
1 of Tag B

2. Trace tree (Pattern Page N) onto the paper side of fusible web; cut out.

3. With fusible side down, press fusible-web shape onto back side of green print. Cut out tree on the lines.

4. Remove paper from fusible-web tree. Place on white felt; press. Carefully cut around tree, leaving 3 mm of white felt showing around tree.

5. Following manufacturer's instructions and aligning raw edges, fuse interfacing to wrong side of tag front. Topstitch tree to right side of tag front using white sewing thread.

6. Sew sequins to tree front and star sequin to top of tree using white sewing thread. **Note:** To secure sequins, make stitches through the center and over the front of the sequin to resemble spokes.

7. Fold ribbon in half with printed side facing out; press fold. With right sides together, sew tag front and tag back, leaving a 2-inch opening along right side and inserting folded ribbon in left side seam. Trim the curves; press. Turn right side out and hand-stitch the opening closed. Topstitch around the edges of the tag.

8. Following manufacturer's instructions, attach a grommet to the center top of the tag. Tie baker's twine through the grommet for a hanger.

Basics & Patterns

Instead of paying a hefty price for custom home decor, learn simple sewing skills so you can make it yourself.

090
gather materials

Like any DIY project, sewing is easier when you have the right tools. Collect these items in a basic sewing kit.

Tape Measure: (A) Measure dimensional objects, such as pillows, with plastic or fabric tape.

Cutting Mat: (B) Use a self-healing mat to protect your work surface when using a rotary cutter.

Fabric Shears: (C) Reserve one pair of shears for fabric only—no paper cutting allowed.

Iron: (D) Keep an iron ready when sewing for crisp hems and seams.

Hand-sewing Needles: (E) Stock an assortment and replace when dull.

Needle Threader: (F) This handy little tool helps with the tricky task of guiding thread through the needle.

Rotary Cutter: (G) This pizza cutter look-alike cuts through fabric layers.

Sewing Gauge: (H) Use this metal ruler to double-check seam allowances when sewing or hem measurements when pressing.

Water-Soluble Markers: (I) Marks made with these are removed with water (don't iron over the marks—they may become permanent).

Seam Ripper: (J) Rip out seams and stitches when the need arises.

Embroidery Scissors: (K) Clip threads and seam allowances with small sharp scissors.

Glass-head Pins: (L) Unlike plastic-head pins, these won't melt when touched by a hot iron.

Pin Cushion: (M) Keep one on hand to keep your pins and needles tidy

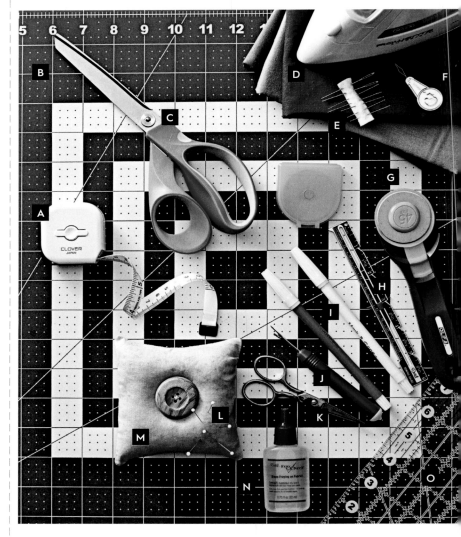

and handy. Magnetic pin cushions will help to find stray pins hiding on the on floors and carpets.

Seam Sealant: (N) Prevent raw edges or knots from fraying with this clear liquid.

Acrylic Ruler: (O) Roll a rotary cutter along a ruler to get straight edges and protect your fingers.

Note: After you've put together a basic sewing kit, you might consider

creating a design wall or board. Having an area to lay out fabric choices or quilt block pieces can help you organize and visualize how they will look in your next project. For a permanent design wall, cover a surface of foam-core board with a napped material, such as flannel or batting. Some sewers use the flannel back of oilcloth or a flannel-backed tablecloth for a design wall, rolling it up between projects.

091
know your fabric types

Fabric stores offer materials in all sorts of weights and textures. Here are some of the most common.

Upholstery Weight: (A) Use this heavier home decor fabric for slipcovers and cushions.

Linen/Linenlike: (B) Linen blends offer the look and lightweight feel of linen without the high price and tendency to wrinkle.

Sheer: (C) For a little privacy without blocking sunlight, use sheer fabrics for drapes.

Faux Suede: (D) This synthetic fabric is tough but still soft, and a good choice for upholstery.

Home Decor Canvas: (E) Can be used for drapes, pillows, and most anything. Available in a wide array of prints and weights.

Velvet: (F) Natural or synthetic velvet offers a luxe look and feel.

Cotton: (G) Medium-weight cotton solids and prints are a great option for decor and apparel projects.

Wool/Woven: (H) Weaves such as classic herringbone or nubby twills add texture and structure.

Knit: (I) For comfort and versatility, try sewing with comfy, stretchy knits.

Outdoor: (J) These fabrics have a finish that makes them water-resistant and/or less susceptible to sun damage.

know your embroidery stitches

Refer to these diagrams and instructions for the embroidery stitches used in the projects in this book.

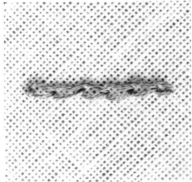

CROSS-STITCH

Gaining popularity from charted designs stitched on uniform squares of Aida cloth, cross-stitch works well for free-form embroidery on other fabrics as well. It's simply two straight stitches crossed at the centers.

To cross-stitch, pull the needle up at A. Insert it back into the fabric at B, bring it up at C, and push the needle down again at D.

CHAIN STITCH

Versatile as a decorative stitch, outline, or border, this stitch is a series of joined loops that resemble a chain.

To chain-stitch, pull the needle up at A, form a U shape with the floss, and hold the shape in place with your thumb. Push the needle back into the fabric at B, about ⅛ inch from A, and come up at C. Repeat for as many chain stitches as desired.

LAZY DAISY STITCH

One loop, similar to the chain stitch, is tacked down with a tiny straight stitch.

To make a lazy daisy stitch, pull the needle up at A and form a loop of floss on the surface. Holding loop in place, insert needle back into fabric at B, about ¹⁄₁₆ inch away from A. Bring needle tip out at C and cross it over the trailing floss, keeping the floss flat. Pull needle and trailing floss until loop lies flat against the fabric. Push the needle through to the back at D to secure the loop.

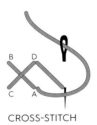

CROSS-STITCH

CHAIN STITCH

LAZY DAISY STITCH

BLANKET STITCH

This decorative stitch can be a bit confusing at first, but with a little practice, you'll pick up the overlapping pattern and stitch with ease.

To blanket-stitch, pull the needle up at A, form a reverse L shape with the floss, and hold the angle of the L shape in place with your thumb. Push the needle down into the fabric at B and come up at C to secure the stitch. Repeat for as many blanket stitches as desired.

OFFSET BACKSTITCH

A variation of the traditional backstitch, this decorative stitch consists of backstitches that are slightly staggered.

To offset-backstitch, pull the needle up at A, insert it back into the fabric at B, and bring it up at C, slightly to the left or right of the first stitch. Push the needle back down into fabric at D in a straight line with C. Continue making stitches that alternate left and right.

FRENCH KNOT

This raised knot makes a nice dimensional accent when stitched alone, sprinkled throughout a design, or grouped to fill a space.

To make a French knot, bring the needle up at A. Wrap the floss around the needle two or three times without twisting it. Insert the needle back into the fabric at B, about 1/16 inch away from A. Gently push the wraps down the needle to meet the fabric, then pull the needle and floss through the fabric slowly and smoothly.

BLANKET STITCH

OFFSET BACKSTITCH

FRENCH KNOT

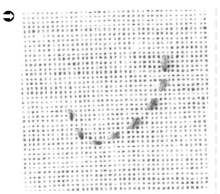

RUNNING STITCH

A simple stitch for borders and outlines, this stitch resembles a dashed line.

To make a running stitch, pull the needle up at A and insert it back into the fabric at B. Continue in the same manner, loading several stitches on the needle at a time. Leave about a stitch width between stitches.

BACKSTITCH

The ideal stitch for outlines, this simple stitch works best when a precise line is necessary.

To backstitch, pull the needle up at A, insert it back into the fabric at B, and bring it up at C. Continue in a straight line or follow an outline.

STRAIGHT STITCH

Sometimes all you need is a basic straight stitch, one stitch, stitched in any direction.

To straight-stitch, pull the needle up at A. Insert needle back into the fabric at B. Continue in the same manner.

RUNNING STITCH

BACKSTITCH

STRAIGHT STITCH

SATIN STITCH

To fill an area with solid stitching, the satin stitch is the perfect choice and is recognized by its closely spaced straight stitches.

To satin-stitch, fill in the design area with straight stitches, stitching from edge to edge and placing stitches side by side.

SATIN STITCH

093
understand quilting basics

MAKE TEMPLATES

A template is a pattern made from extra-sturdy material so you can trace around it many times without wearing away the edges. Acrylic templates for many common shapes are available at quilt shops. Or make your own by duplicating printed patterns on template plastic.

To make permanent templates, purchase easy-to-cut template plastic, available at quilt shops and crafts supply stores. Lay the plastic over a printed pattern. Trace the pattern onto the plastic using a ruler and a permanent marker to ensure straight lines, accurate corners, and permanency (A).

For hand piecing and appliqué, make templates the exact size finished pieces will be (without seam allowances). For piecing, this means tracing the patterns' dashed lines.

For machine piecing, make templates that include seam allowances by tracing the patterns' solid and dashed lines onto the template plastic (B).

For easy reference, mark each template with its letter designation, grain line (if noted on the pattern), and block or project name. Also mark the matching point of each corner on the seam line (these may be indicated with dots on the printed pattern). Cut out the traced shapes on their outside lines. Using a pushpin, make a hole in the template at each corner matching point (C). The hole must be large enough for the point of a pencil or marking pen to mark through (D).

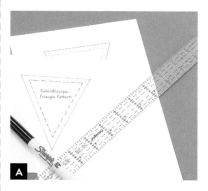

A

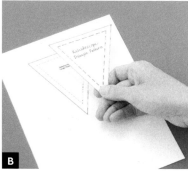

B

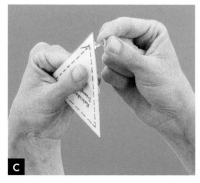

C

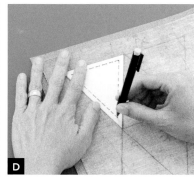

D

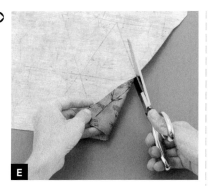

E

F

G

Verify each template's shape and size by placing it over its printed pattern. Templates must be accurate because errors, however small, compound many times as you assemble a project. To check templates' accuracy, make a test block before cutting the fabric pieces for an entire project.

USE TEMPLATES

To trace a template on fabric, use a pencil, a white dressmaker's pencil, chalk, or a special fabric marker that makes a thin, accurate line. Do not use a ballpoint or ink pen; the lines may bleed if washed. Test all marking tools on a fabric scrap before using them.

To make pieces for hand piecing, place a template facedown on the wrong side of the fabric and trace. If desired, mark the matching points on the corners of the seam lines. To make pieces for hand appliqué, place a template faceup on the right side of the fabric and trace. Reposition template at least ½ inch away from previous tracing, trace again, and repeat. The lines you trace on the fabric are the sewing lines.

Mark cutting lines ¼ inch away from the sewing lines or estimate the distance by eye when cutting out pieces with scissors. For hand piecing, add a ¼-inch seam allowance; for hand appliqué, add a ³⁄₁₆-inch seam allowance.

Because templates used to make pieces for machine piecing have seam allowances included, you can use common tracing lines for efficient cutting. Place a template facedown on the wrong side of the fabric and trace. Mark corner matching points through holes in template; they should each be right on the seam line. Reposition template without leaving a space between it and the previous tracing, trace again, and repeat. Using scissors or a rotary cutter and ruler, cut out pieces, cutting precisely on the drawn lines (E).

CUT BIAS STRIPS

Strips for curved appliqué pieces and for binding curved edges should be cut on the bias, which runs at a 45° angle to the selvages (or diagonally across the grain of a woven fabric) and has the most

stretch (Bias Strip Diagram). Directional fabrics also can be cut on the bias for purely visual reasons.

To cut bias strips, begin with a fabric square or rectangle; use an acrylic ruler to square up the left edge if necessary. Make a cut at a 45° angle to the left edge. Handle the diagonal edges carefully to avoid distorting the bias. To cut a strip, measure the desired width from the 45° cut edge; cut parallel to the edge (F). Cut enough strips to total the length needed.

COMPLETE QUILT

Cut and piece backing fabric to measure at least 4 inches bigger on all sides than the quilt top. (For quilts smaller than 20 inches, our instructions specify batting and backing only 3 inches bigger on all sides.) Press seams open. With wrong sides together, layer quilt top and backing fabric with the batting in between; baste. Quilt as desired. Trim the batting and backing fabric even with the quilt top edges; machine-baste a scant ¼ inch from quilt top edges if desired. (Some quilters prefer to wait until they have

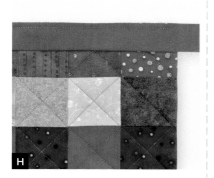

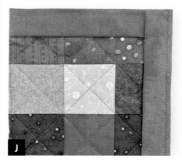

machine-sewn the binding to the quilt top before trimming the batting and backing.) Binding for most quilts is cut on the straight grain of the fabric. If your quilt has curved edges, cut strips on the bias. Cutting instructions for projects specify the number of binding strips or a total length needed to finish the quilt. Instructions also specify enough width for a French-fold, or double-layer, binding because it's easier to apply and adds durability.

Join strips with diagonal seams to make one continuous binding strip (G). Trim excess fabric, leaving ¼-inch seam allowances. Press seams open. Fold one end of the binding strip under 1 inch; press. With wrong side inside, fold strip in half lengthwise and press.

Beginning in the center of one edge and using folded end of binding strip, place binding strip against right side of quilt top, aligning binding strip's raw edges with quilt top's raw edge (H). Begin sewing the binding in place through all layers 2 inches from the folded end, stopping ¼ inch (or distance equal to the seam allowance you're using)

from the corner. Backstitch, then clip threads. Remove quilt from under the sewing-machine presser foot.

Fold binding strip upward, creating a diagonal fold; finger-press (I).

Holding diagonal fold in place with your finger, bring binding strip down in line with next edge of quilt top, making a horizontal fold that aligns with the quilt edge (J).

Start sewing again at top of horizontal fold, stitching through all layers. Sew around quilt, turning each corner in the same manner.

When you return to the starting

point, encase binding strip's raw edge inside the folded end. Finish sewing to starting point. Trim batting and backing fabric even with quilt top edges if not done earlier.

Turn binding over each edge to the quilt back. Hand-stitch binding to backing fabric, making sure to cover all machine stitching.

To make mitered corners on quilt back, hand-stitch up to a corner; fold a miter in the binding. Take a stitch or two in the fold to secure it. Then stitch the binding in place up to the next corner. Finish each corner in the same manner.

BIAS STRIP DIAGRAM

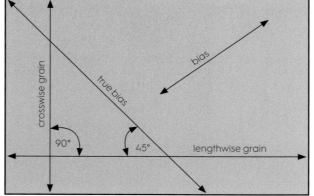

094
get binding basics

CUT THE STRIPS

Refer to project instructions for the width and number of binding strips to cut. Unless otherwise specified, cut binding strips on the straight grain of the fabric.

To determine the number of binding strips you need to cut, measure the sides of your quilt, add 12", then divide by the width of your binding fabric. For a 40" by 55" quilt, that has binding cut from 42" wide fabric:

40" + 40" + 55" + 55" + 12" = 202"
202" / 42" = 4.8 strips, rounded up to 5.

If you are using scraps to piece together a binding, use the first part of the calculation to determine the final total length you will need.

Place strips perpendicular to each other and join binding strips with diagonal seams (below) to make one long binding strip. Trim seams to ¼ inch; press open.

ATTACH THE BINDING

With the wrong side inside, fold under 1 inch at one end of the binding strip and press. Then press the strip in half lengthwise with the wrong side inside. Place the binding strip against the right side of the quilt top along one edge, aligning the binding strip's raw edges with the quilt top's raw edge (do not start at a corner). Begin sewing the binding in place 2 inches from the folded end.

TURN THE CORNER

Stop sewing when you're ¼ inch from the corner (or a distance equal to the seam allowance you're using). Backstitch, then clip the threads (A). Remove the quilt from under sewing-machine presser foot.

Fold the binding strip upward, creating a diagonal fold, and finger-press (B).

Holding the diagonal fold in place with your finger, bring the binding strip down in line with the next edge, making a horizontal fold that aligns with the quilt edge. Start sewing again at the top of the horizontal fold, stitching through all layers (C). Sew around the quilt, turning each corner the same way.

FINISH IT

When you return to the starting point, encase the binding strip's raw edge inside the folded end and finish sewing to the starting point. Trim the batting and backing fabric even with the quilt top edges if not done earlier.

Turn the binding over the edge to the back. Hand-stitch the binding to the backing fabric only, covering the machine stitching. To make the binding corners on the quilt back, match the mitered corners on the quilt front, hand-stitch up to a corner, and make a fold in the binding. Secure fold with a couple stitches, then continue stitching the binding in place along the next edge.

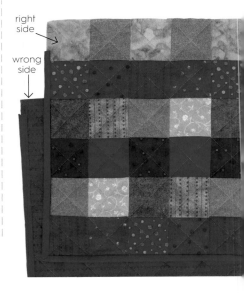

right side

wrong side

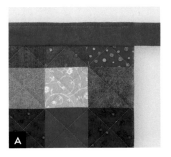

A

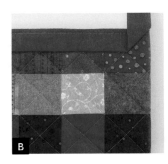

B

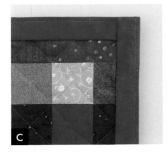

C

Patterns

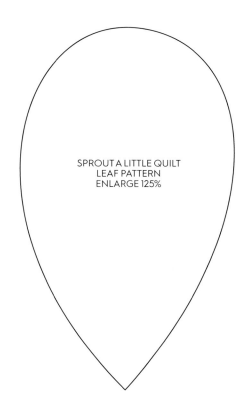

QUILT MODERN POT HOLDERS
CORNER CUTTING PATTERN
ENLARGE 200%

SPROUT A LITTLE QUILT
LEAF PATTERN
ENLARGE 125%

PACK SUPERIOR SNACKS
LARGE SNACK BAG PATTERN
ENLARGE 750%

8.75"	8.75"
7.25"	7.25"
8.75"	8.75"
7.25"	7.25"

18"

21"

PACK SUPERIOR SNACKS
SMALL SNACK BAG PATTERN
ENLARGE 750%

6.25"	6.25"	6.25"
6.75"	6.75"	6.75"
6.25"	6.25"	6.25"
6.75"	6.75"	6.75"

18"

21"

B

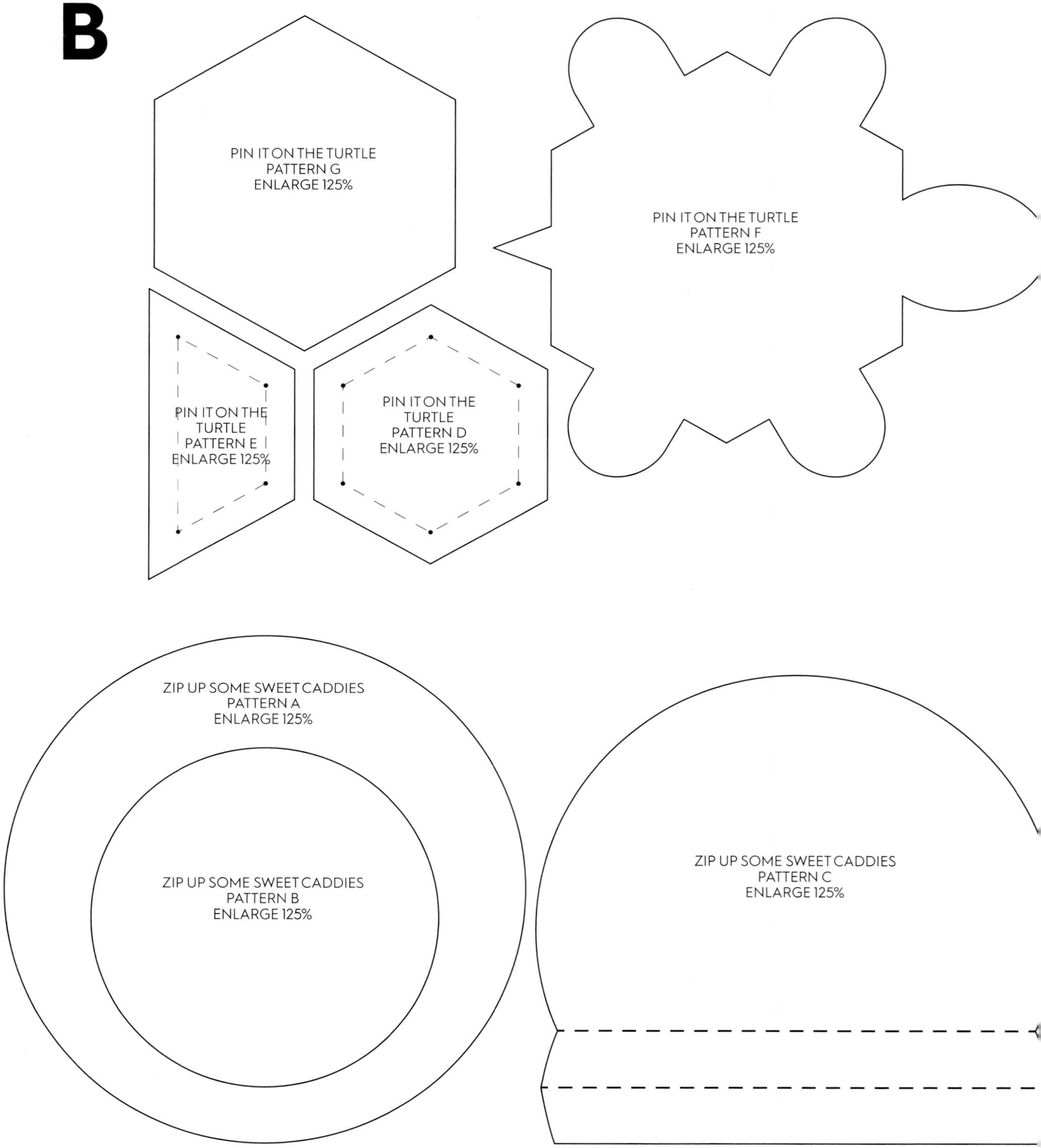

PIN IT ON THE TURTLE
PATTERN G
ENLARGE 125%

PIN IT ON THE TURTLE
PATTERN F
ENLARGE 125%

PIN IT ON THE
TURTLE
PATTERN E
ENLARGE 125%

PIN IT ON THE
TURTLE
PATTERN D
ENLARGE 125%

ZIP UP SOME SWEET CADDIES
PATTERN A
ENLARGE 125%

ZIP UP SOME SWEET CADDIES
PATTERN B
ENLARGE 125%

ZIP UP SOME SWEET CADDIES
PATTERN C
ENLARGE 125%

C

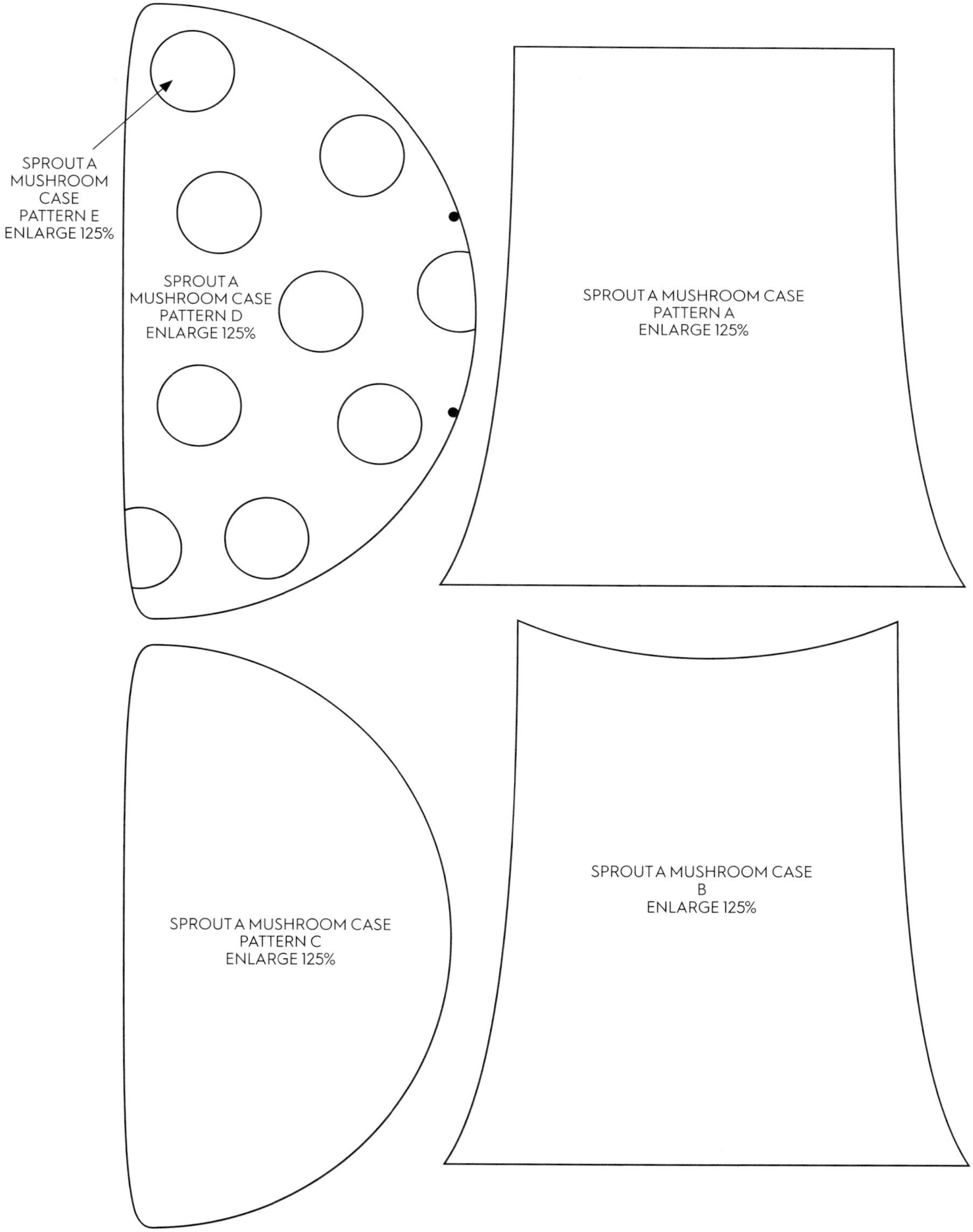

SPROUT A
MUSHROOM
CASE
PATTERN E
ENLARGE 125%

SPROUT A
MUSHROOM CASE
PATTERN D
ENLARGE 125%

SPROUT A MUSHROOM CASE
PATTERN A
ENLARGE 125%

SPROUT A MUSHROOM CASE
PATTERN C
ENLARGE 125%

SPROUT A MUSHROOM CASE
B
ENLARGE 125%

D

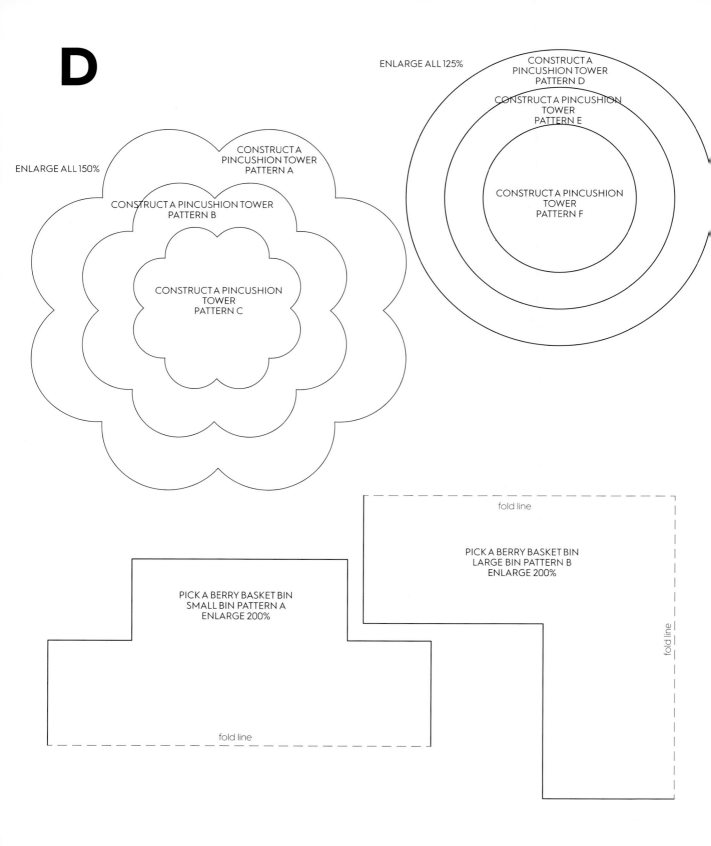

ENLARGE ALL 125%

CONSTRUCT A
PINCUSHION TOWER
PATTERN D

CONSTRUCT A PINCUSHION
TOWER
PATTERN E

CONSTRUCT A PINCUSHION
TOWER
PATTERN F

ENLARGE ALL 150%

CONSTRUCT A
PINCUSHION TOWER
PATTERN A

CONSTRUCT A PINCUSHION TOWER
PATTERN B

CONSTRUCT A PINCUSHION
TOWER
PATTERN C

fold line

PICK A BERRY BASKET BIN
LARGE BIN PATTERN B
ENLARGE 200%

PICK A BERRY BASKET BIN
SMALL BIN PATTERN A
ENLARGE 200%

fold line

fold line

E

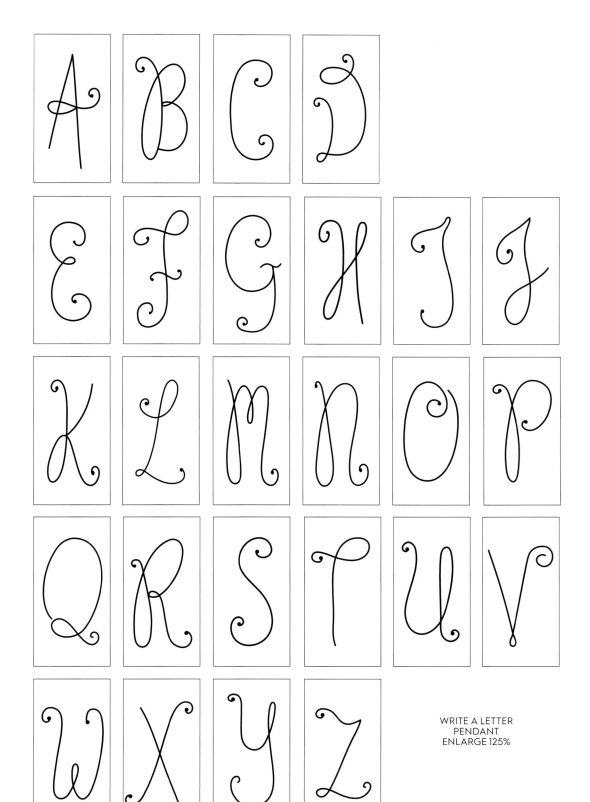

WRITE A LETTER
PENDANT
ENLARGE 125%

F

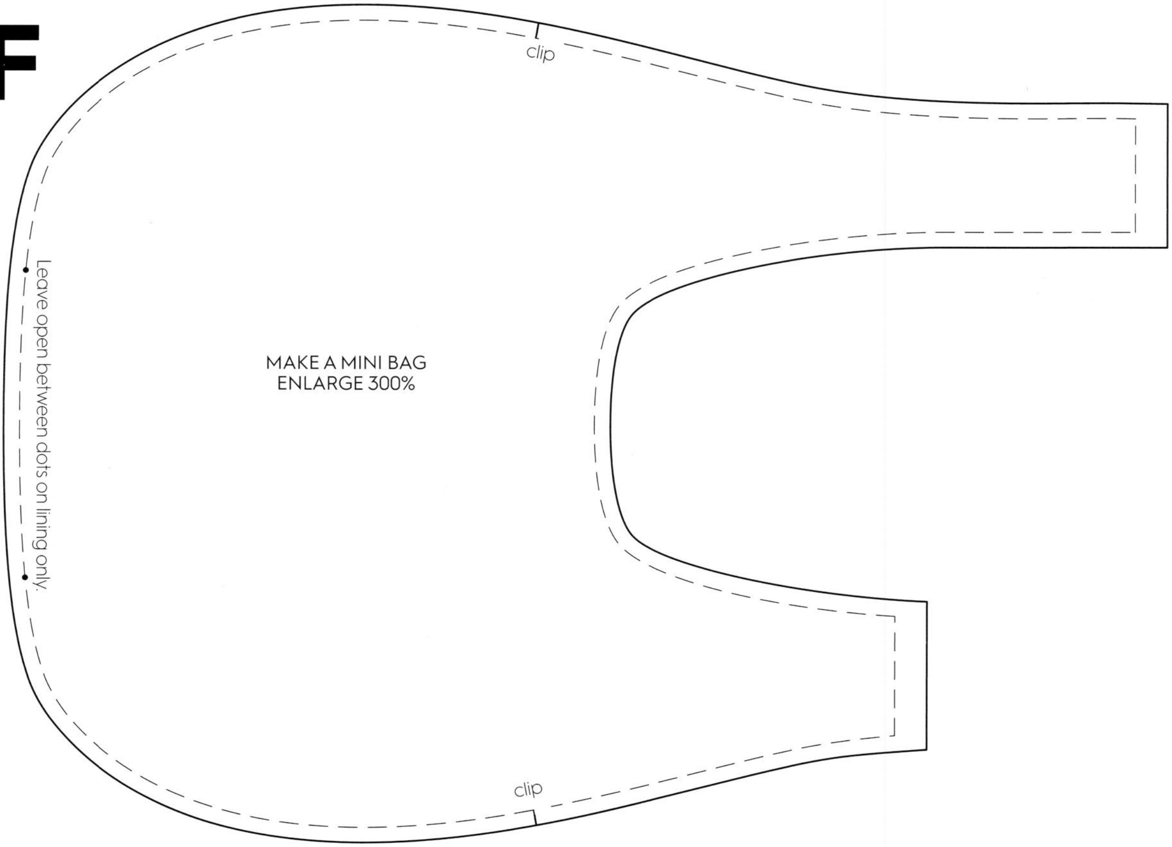

MAKE A MINI BAG
ENLARGE 300%

Leave open between dots on lining only.

clip

clip

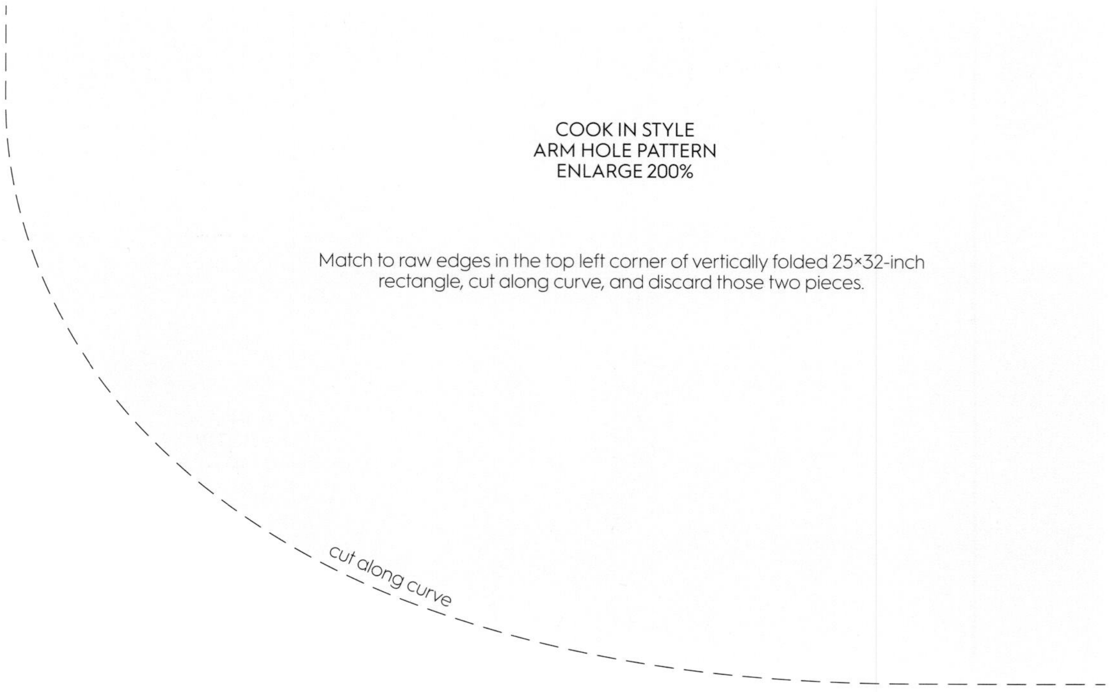

COOK IN STYLE
ARM HOLE PATTERN
ENLARGE 200%

Match to raw edges in the top left corner of vertically folded 25×32-inch
rectangle, cut along curve, and discard those two pieces.

cut along curve

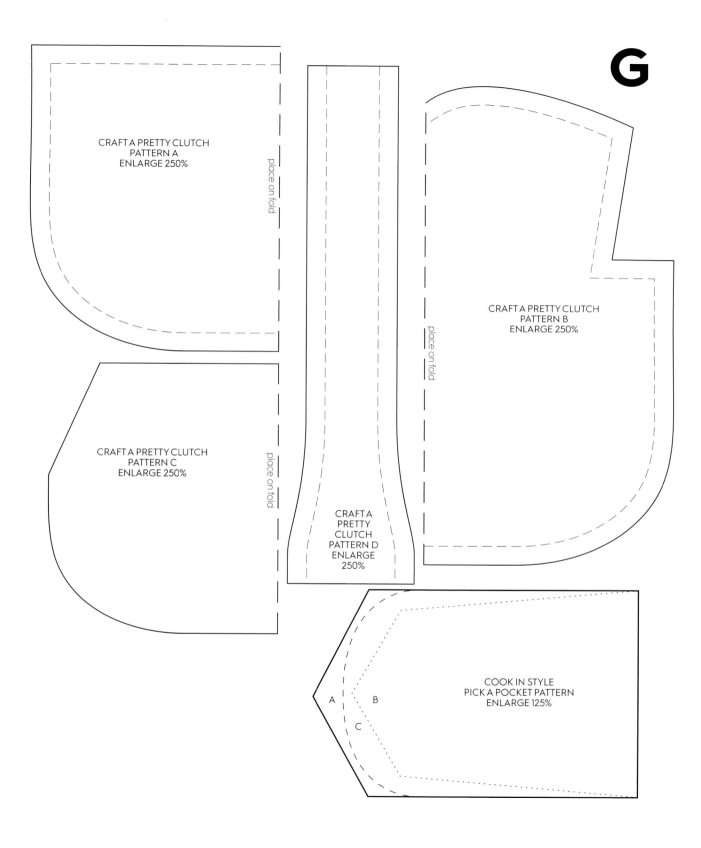

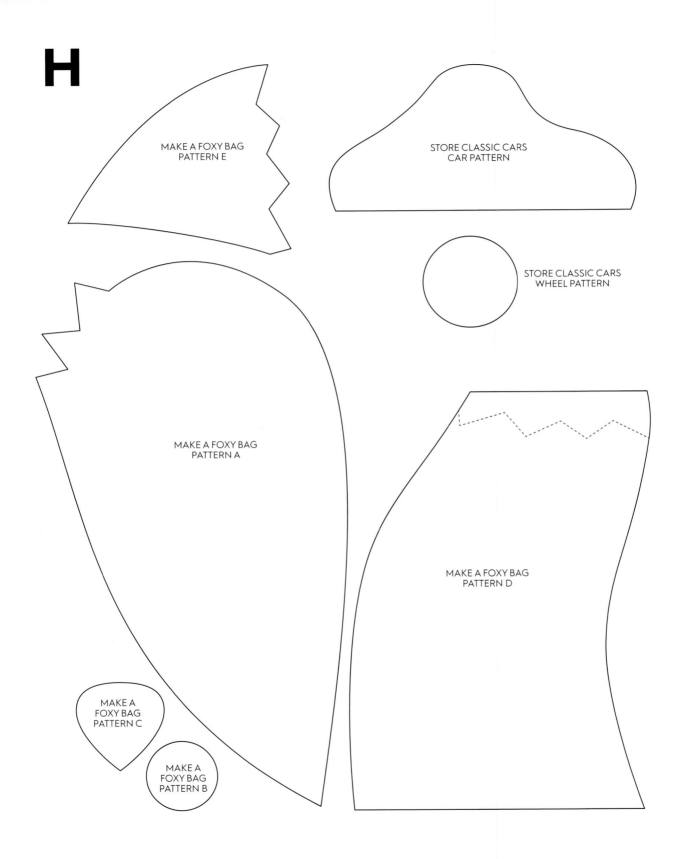

H

MAKE A FOXY BAG
PATTERN E

STORE CLASSIC CARS
CAR PATTERN

STORE CLASSIC CARS
WHEEL PATTERN

MAKE A FOXY BAG
PATTERN A

MAKE A FOXY BAG
PATTERN D

MAKE A
FOXY BAG
PATTERN C

MAKE A
FOXY BAG
PATTERN B

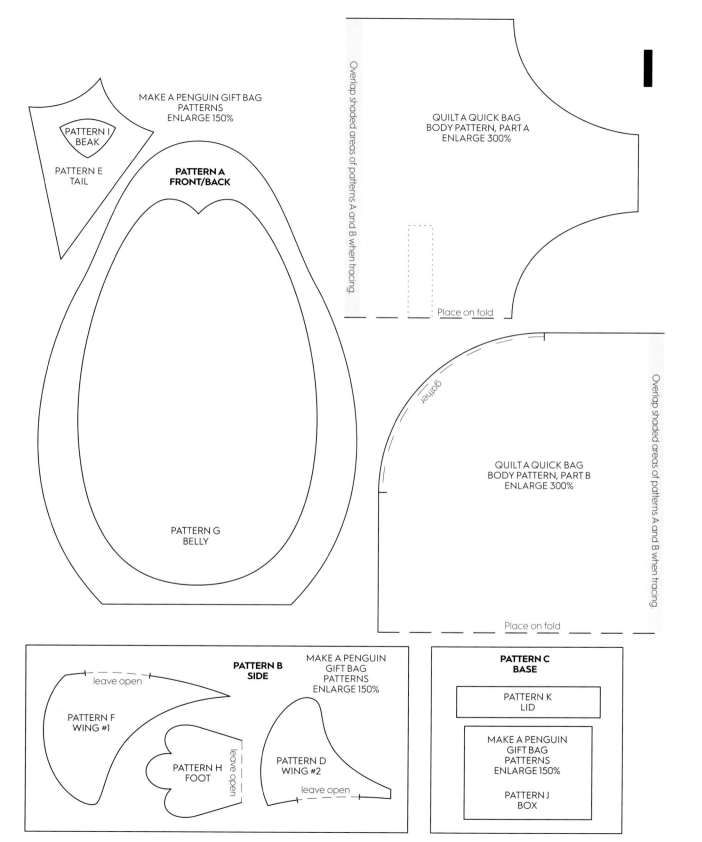

MAKE A PENGUIN GIFT BAG
PATTERNS
ENLARGE 150%

PATTERN I
BEAK

PATTERN E
TAIL

PATTERN A
FRONT/BACK

PATTERN G
BELLY

QUILT A QUICK BAG
BODY PATTERN, PART A
ENLARGE 300%

Overlap shaded areas of patterns A and B when tracing

Place on fold

gather

QUILT A QUICK BAG
BODY PATTERN, PART B
ENLARGE 300%

Overlap shaded areas of patterns A and B when tracing

Place on fold

PATTERN B
SIDE

MAKE A PENGUIN
GIFT BAG
PATTERNS
ENLARGE 150%

leave open

PATTERN F
WING #1

PATTERN H
FOOT

leave open

PATTERN D
WING #2

leave open

PATTERN C
BASE

PATTERN K
LID

MAKE A PENGUIN
GIFT BAG
PATTERNS
ENLARGE 150%

PATTERN J
BOX

J

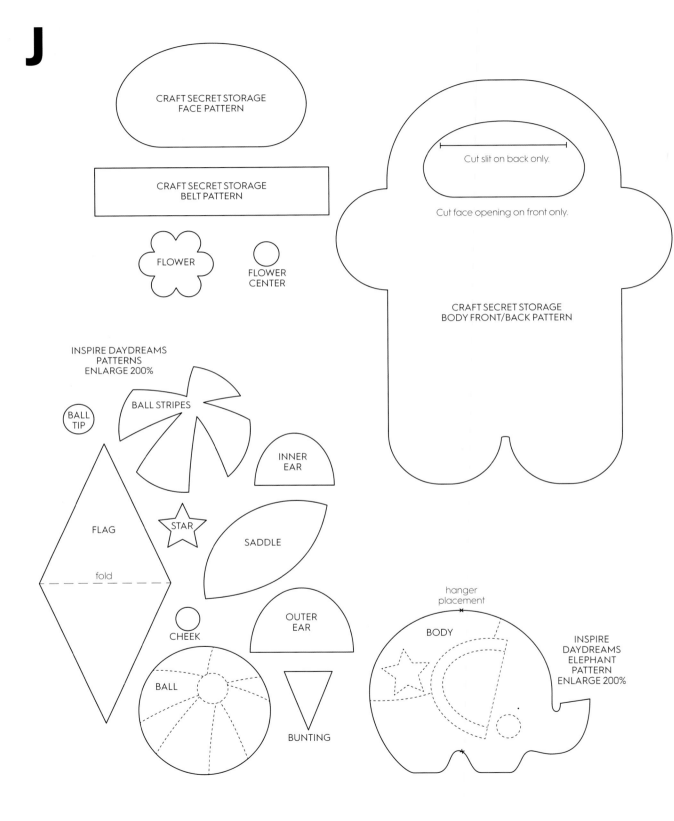

CRAFT SECRET STORAGE
FACE PATTERN

CRAFT SECRET STORAGE
BELT PATTERN

FLOWER

FLOWER
CENTER

Cut slit on back only.

Cut face opening on front only.

CRAFT SECRET STORAGE
BODY FRONT/BACK PATTERN

INSPIRE DAYDREAMS
PATTERNS
ENLARGE 200%

BALL
TIP

BALL STRIPES

INNER
EAR

FLAG

STAR

SADDLE

fold

CHEEK

OUTER
EAR

BALL

BUNTING

hanger
placement

BODY

INSPIRE
DAYDREAMS
ELEPHANT
PATTERN
ENLARGE 200%

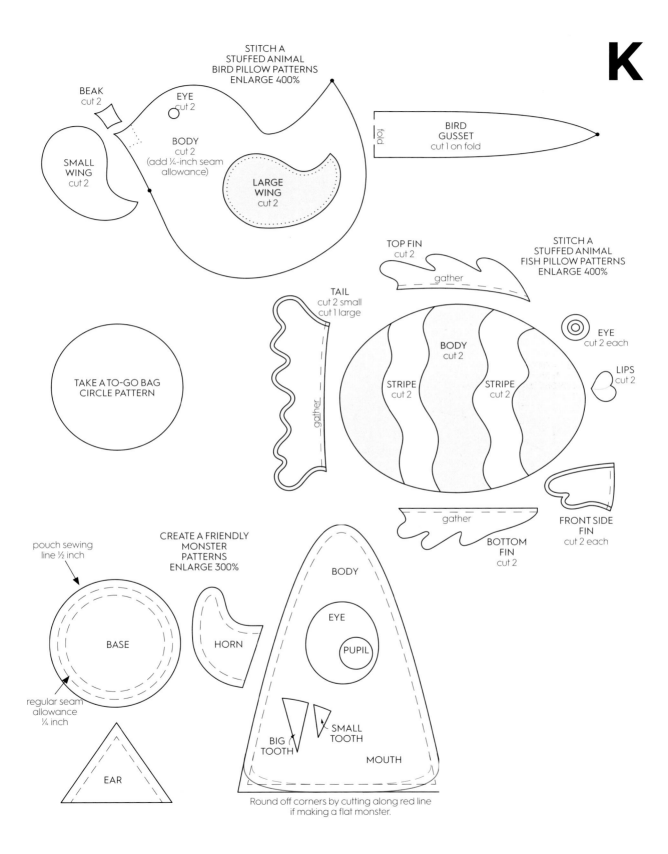

K

STITCH A
STUFFED ANIMAL
BIRD PILLOW PATTERNS
ENLARGE 400%

BEAK
cut 2

EYE
cut 2

SMALL
WING
cut 2

BODY
cut 2
(add ¼-inch seam
allowance)

LARGE
WING
cut 2

fold

BIRD
GUSSET
cut 1 on fold

TOP FIN
cut 2

gather

STITCH A
STUFFED ANIMAL
FISH PILLOW PATTERNS
ENLARGE 400%

TAIL
cut 2 small
cut 1 large

gather

EYE
cut 2 each

BODY
cut 2

STRIPE
cut 2

STRIPE
cut 2

LIPS
cut 2

TAKE A TO-GO BAG
CIRCLE PATTERN

gather

BOTTOM
FIN
cut 2

FRONT SIDE
FIN
cut 2 each

CREATE A FRIENDLY
MONSTER
PATTERNS
ENLARGE 300%

pouch sewing
line ½ inch

BASE

regular seam
allowance
¼ inch

HORN

BODY

EYE

PUPIL

BIG
TOOTH

SMALL
TOOTH

MOUTH

EAR

Round off corners by cutting along red line
if making a flat monster.

L

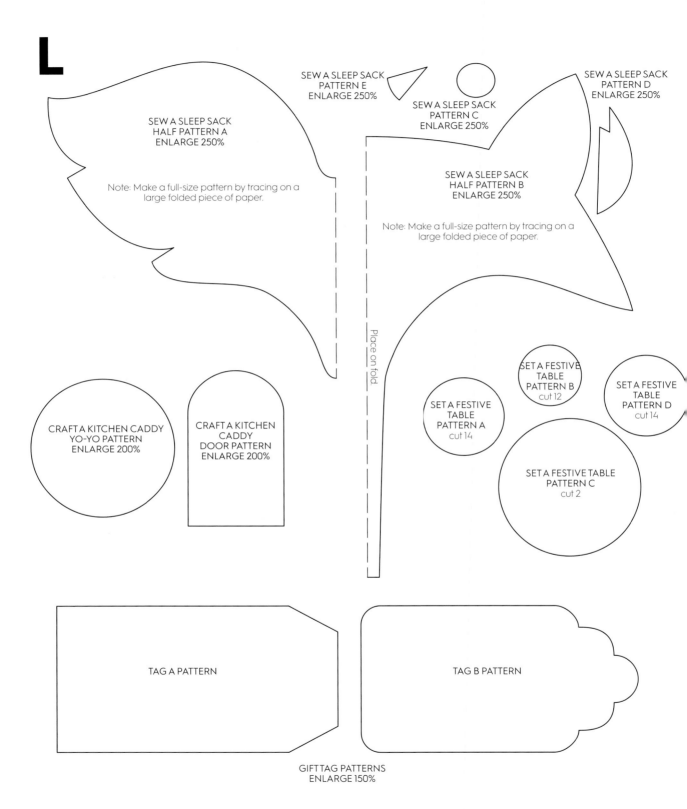

SEW A SLEEP SACK
HALF PATTERN A
ENLARGE 250%

Note: Make a full-size pattern by tracing on a
large folded piece of paper.

SEW A SLEEP SACK
PATTERN E
ENLARGE 250%

SEW A SLEEP SACK
PATTERN C
ENLARGE 250%

SEW A SLEEP SACK
PATTERN D
ENLARGE 250%

SEW A SLEEP SACK
HALF PATTERN B
ENLARGE 250%

Note: Make a full-size pattern by tracing on a
large folded piece of paper.

Place on fold

CRAFT A KITCHEN CADDY
YO-YO PATTERN
ENLARGE 200%

CRAFT A KITCHEN
CADDY
DOOR PATTERN
ENLARGE 200%

SET A FESTIVE
TABLE
PATTERN B
cut 12

SET A FESTIVE
TABLE
PATTERN D
cut 14

SET A FESTIVE
TABLE
PATTERN A
cut 14

SET A FESTIVE TABLE
PATTERN C
cut 2

TAG A PATTERN

TAG B PATTERN

GIFT TAG PATTERNS
ENLARGE 150%

cookies

SEW A SNACK MAT
FOR SANTA
ENLARGE 150%

milk

SEW A SNACK MAT
FOR SANTA
ENLARGE 150%

M

WHIP UP A HOLIDAY
HOT PAD
WORD PATTERNS

SEW A SNACK MAT
FOR SANTA
ENLARGE 150%

crumbs

STRING MINI MITTENS
PATTERN

WHIP UP A HOLIDAY
HOT PAD
GINGERBREAD BOY
PATTERN

You are what you eat
So eat something sweet

TAG IT WITH A TREAT
PATTERN

HAT
CROWN

HAT
BRIM

MAKE A SPECIAL DELIVERY
LETTERING

Special Delivery

PUT A POINSETTIA ON IT
LARGE POINSETTIA
PATTERN

PUT A POINSETTIA ON IT
MEDIUM POINSETTIA
PATTERN

PUT A POINSETTIA ON IT
SMALL POINSETTIA
PATTERN

MAKE A SPECIAL
DELIVERY
BIRD PATTERN

DRESS A PACKAGE
WITH A REINDEER
PATTERN

TRIM WITH A TREE
PATTERN

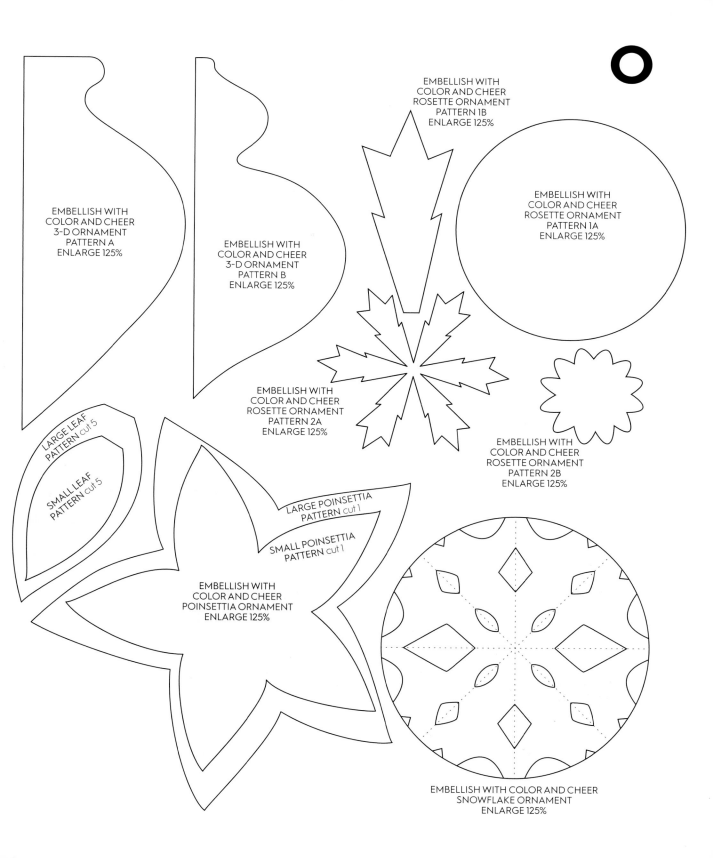

EMBELLISH WITH COLOR AND CHEER
3-D ORNAMENT PATTERN A
ENLARGE 125%

EMBELLISH WITH COLOR AND CHEER
3-D ORNAMENT PATTERN B
ENLARGE 125%

EMBELLISH WITH COLOR AND CHEER
ROSETTE ORNAMENT PATTERN 1B
ENLARGE 125%

EMBELLISH WITH COLOR AND CHEER
ROSETTE ORNAMENT PATTERN 1A
ENLARGE 125%

EMBELLISH WITH COLOR AND CHEER
ROSETTE ORNAMENT PATTERN 2A
ENLARGE 125%

EMBELLISH WITH COLOR AND CHEER
ROSETTE ORNAMENT PATTERN 2B
ENLARGE 125%

LARGE LEAF PATTERN cut 5

SMALL LEAF PATTERN cut 5

LARGE POINSETTIA PATTERN cut 1

SMALL POINSETTIA PATTERN cut 1

EMBELLISH WITH COLOR AND CHEER
POINSETTIA ORNAMENT
ENLARGE 125%

EMBELLISH WITH COLOR AND CHEER
SNOWFLAKE ORNAMENT
ENLARGE 125%

P

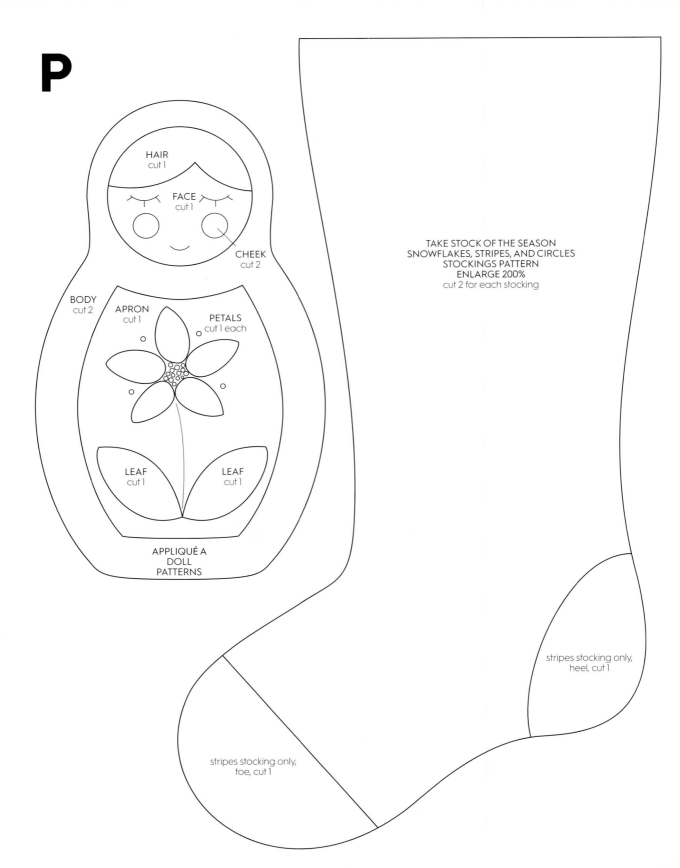

HAIR
cut 1

FACE
cut 1

CHEEK
cut 2

BODY
cut 2

APRON
cut 1

PETALS
cut 1 each

LEAF
cut 1

LEAF
cut 1

APPLIQUÉ A
DOLL
PATTERNS

TAKE STOCK OF THE SEASON
SNOWFLAKES, STRIPES, AND CIRCLES
STOCKINGS PATTERN
ENLARGE 200%
cut 2 for each stocking

stripes stocking only,
heel, cut 1

stripes stocking only,
toe, cut 1

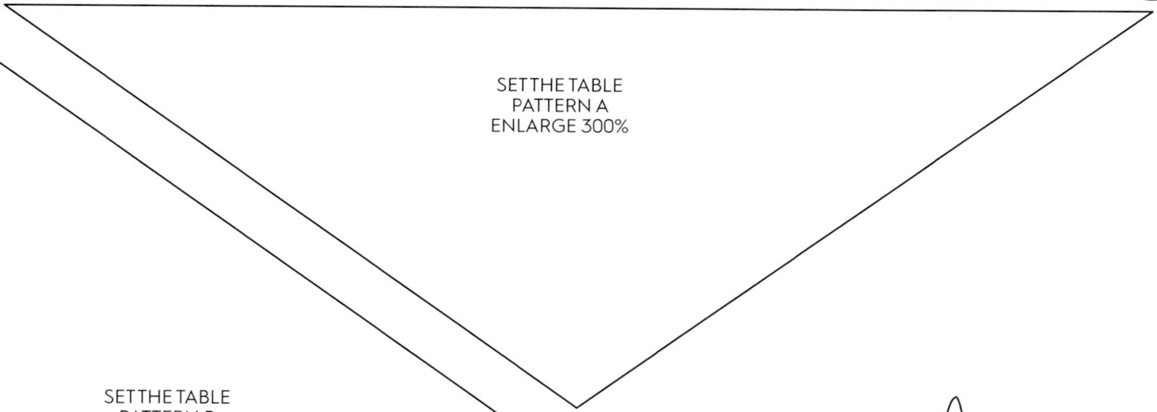

Q

SET THE TABLE
PATTERN A
ENLARGE 300%

SET THE TABLE
PATTERN B
ENLARGE 300%

TAKE STOCK OF THE SEASON
CIRCLES STOCKING
CIRCLES PATTERNS

TAKE STOCK OF THE SEASON
CIRCLES STOCKING
STARS PATTERNS

R

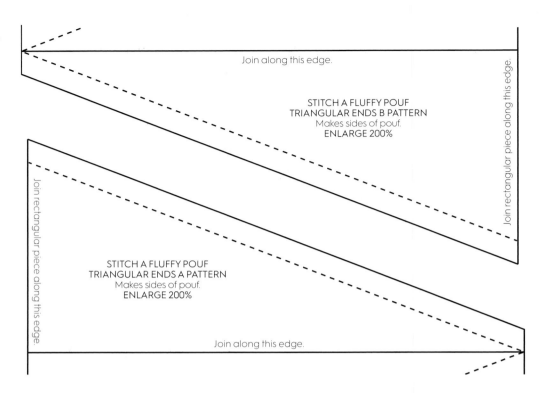

Join along this edge.

Join rectangular piece along this edge.

STITCH A FLUFFY POUF
TRIANGULAR ENDS B PATTERN
Makes sides of pouf.
ENLARGE 200%

Join rectangular piece along this edge.

STITCH A FLUFFY POUF
TRIANGULAR ENDS A PATTERN
Makes sides of pouf.
ENLARGE 200%

Join along this edge.

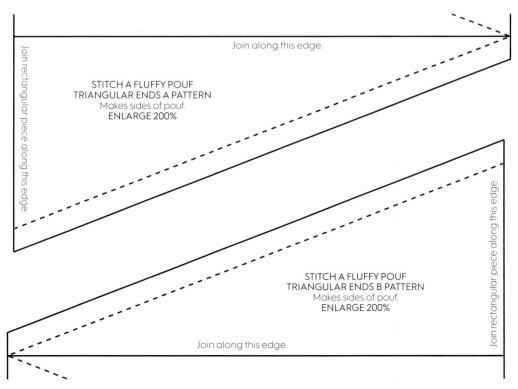

Join along this edge.

Join rectangular piece along this edge.

STITCH A FLUFFY POUF
TRIANGULAR ENDS A PATTERN
Makes sides of pouf.
ENLARGE 200%

STITCH A FLUFFY POUF
TRIANGULAR ENDS B PATTERN
Makes sides of pouf.
ENLARGE 200%

Join rectangular piece along this edge.

Join along this edge.

S

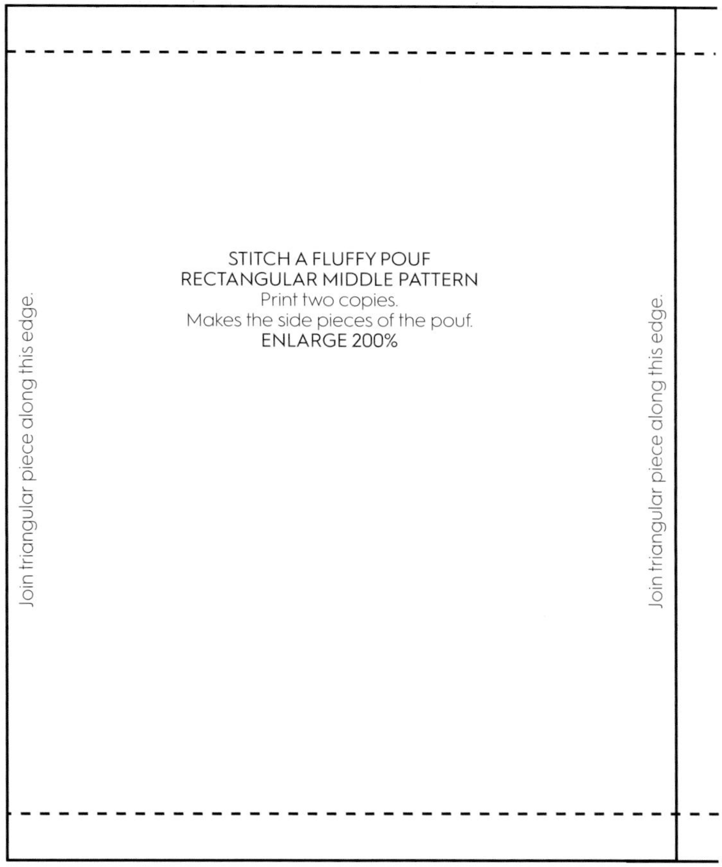

STITCH A FLUFFY POUF
RECTANGULAR MIDDLE PATTERN
Print two copies.
Makes the side pieces of the pouf.
ENLARGE 200%

Join triangular piece along this edge.

Join triangular piece along this edge.

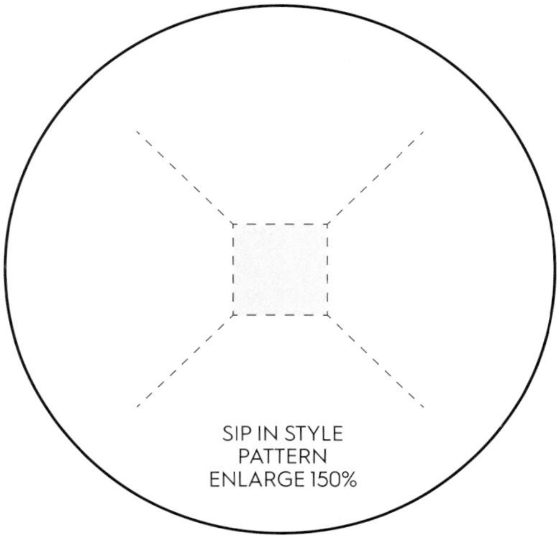

SIP IN STYLE
PATTERN
ENLARGE 150%

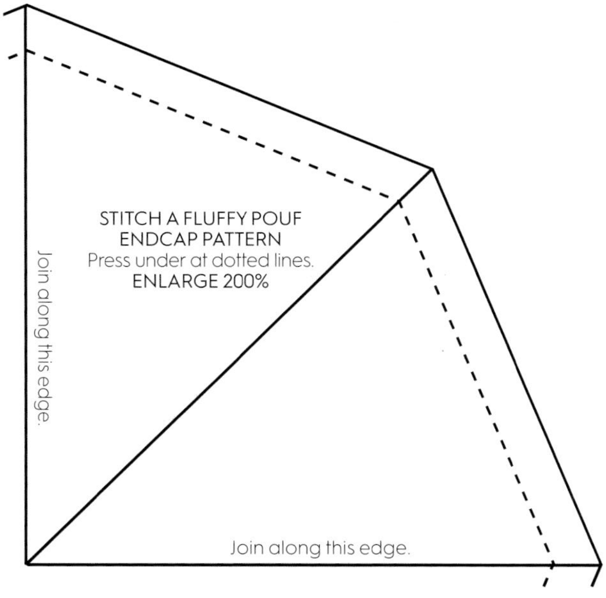

STITCH A FLUFFY POUF
ENDCAP PATTERN
Press under at dotted lines.
ENLARGE 200%

Join along this edge.

Join along this edge.

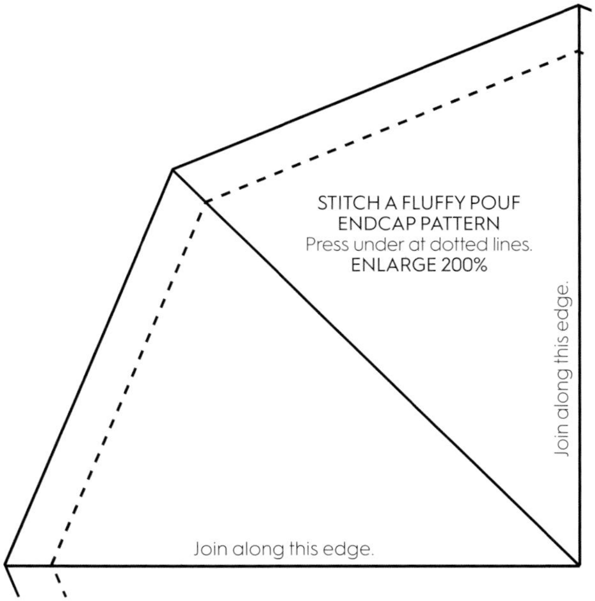

STITCH A FLUFFY POUF
ENDCAP PATTERN
Press under at dotted lines.
ENLARGE 200%

Join along this edge.

Join along this edge.

index

METRIC CONVERSION CHART

IMPERIAL MEASUREMENT	METRIC MEASUREMENT
⅛ inch	3 mm
¼ inch	6 mm
⅜ inch	9.5 mm
½ inch	13 mm
⅝ inch	16 mm
¾ inch	19 mm
1 inch	2.5 cm
1 foot	30. 5 cm
1 yard	0.91 m

weldon**owen**

PRESIDENT & PUBLISHER Roger Shaw
SVP, SALES & MARKETING Amy Kaneko

SENIOR EDITOR Lucie Parker
EDITORIAL ASSISTANT Molly O'Neil Stewart

CREATIVE DIRECTOR Kelly Booth
ART DIRECTOR Lorraine Rath
SENIOR PRODUCTION DESIGNER Rachel Lopez Metzger

ASSOCIATE PRODUCTION DIRECTOR Michelle Duggan
IMAGING MANAGER Don Hill

Waterbury Publications, Inc., Des Moines, IA
CREATIVE DIRECTOR Ken Carlson
EDITORIAL DIRECTOR Lisa Kingsley
SENIOR EDITOR Tricia Bergman
ART DIRECTOR Doug Samuelson
PRODUCTION ASSISTANT Mindy Samuelson

Meredith Core Media
EDITORIAL CONTENT DIRECTOR Doug Kouma
BRAND LEADER Karman Hotchkiss
CREATIVE DIRECTOR Michelle Bilyeu
Business Administration
VICE PRESIDENT/GROUP PUBLISHER Scott Mortimer
EXECUTIVE ACCOUNT DIRECTOR Doug Stark

All content and images courtesy of the Meredith Corporation.

ISBN 978-168188-286-4

10 9 8 7 6 5 4 3 2

2018 2019 2020 2021

Printed in China.